Paintball!
Strategies & Tactics

Revised Edition

PAINTBALL!
STRATEGIES & TACTICS

BILL BARNES

with
Peter Wrenn

Illustrations by
"Scenario" Don Hawthorne

Mustang Publishing
Memphis, TN

Library of Congress CIP data:

Barnes, Bill.
      Paintball! : strategies & tactics / Bill Barnes with Peter Wrenn ; illustrations by "Scenario" Don Hawthorne.
         p. cm.
      Rev. ed. of : The survival game. c1989.
      ISBN: 0-914457-52-7 (alk. paper)
        1. Survival Game. I. Wrenn, Peter. II. Barnes, Bill.
Survival game. III. Title.
GV1202.S87B37   1993
796.1–dc20   93-4012
                                 CIP

Printed on acid-free paper.

10 9 8 7 6 5 4

To my mother and father,
John Edward Barnes and Elizabeth Barnes,
my brother Johnny,
and my sister Shara.

Acknowledgments

I would like to express my deepest, heartfelt thanks and appreciation to the following captains, teammates, field owners, and special friends with whom I have shared the good times while playing paintball:

Tony Mederos, Peter Wrenn, "Scenario" Don Hawthorne and family, "Ninja Bill" and Angel Saugez, Mr. and Mrs. Parker, Jim Murphy, Steve Kisch, Carly Archibeque, Jack Willis, Kevin Dyer, Mike Missile, "Little Joe," Michael and JayAnn Rodgers, Terry and Barbara Hufford and their sons John and Bob, Ross Alexander, Tim Lebay, Henry, J.B., Jerry Yandell, Jessica Sparks, Russell Maynard, Marty Tripes, Marko and Liz Fox, "Possum" Byars, Scott Allen, Dale Bailes, Bruce Joyner, Jim Reardon, Tom Lubin, Fred Munch, Leo and "Nurse Cindy" Orozco and her sister Maggie, The Iceman, The Termite, Rod and Sherri Vanderheydt, Jeff and Susie Biggs, Ben and Mary Ellen Lemberg, Cameron and Vicki Rose, Thor Koole, Rick Dodson, Craig "Sgt. Fatlip" Durst, Mike Keyes, Dave Coennen, Andy Greenwell and his wife Helen, Mike Campbell, and the best overall player I've ever had the pleasure of playing with, Steve "The Mad Hobbit" Pilcher.

And I'd like to thank all the former No Namers not previously mentioned: Allen, Andre, Jim and Bob Long, Chuck, George, Gunn, Gordo, Mike Hutter, Lucas Foster, Kirk, Pat Keyes, Patrick, Anthony, Tom, and Marcie.

Also my teammates (not previously listed) on Navarone: Mark Bower, John "Safety Briefing" Thompson, Lance Skank, Dan Visnaw, Steve Rickman, Mike Gibbons, Jeff Klemm, Bob Schryver, Bill Homa, George Acosta, Mark Christian, Rod Plunkett, Paul Grimmie, Eric Mondragon, Jim Daniels, Richard Yabuki, Roger Oepkes, Gary "Look At My Arm" Miller, Ricky Thom, Bob Tway, Rich Tway, Neal Sullivan, Mike Aguon, John McCloud, Adam Hall, Scott Anderson, Steve Lund, Dan Marquez, Bill Cotter, Rick Rector, Brad Molner, Mick "I Can Guess Your Weight" Gorton, Greg "S. H. Luke" Duran, Cecil Jenkins, Joe Whitcomb, Dave Schoch, John Lenz, and Mike Zacharia.

And to my friends on the Allied Special Forces: Mike Ahauna, Randall Atkins, Ron Betts, Eugene Brown, Jeff Cooke, Jim Gwynn, Charlie Hubbard, Sam King, Guy Miller, Ed Pearson, Steve Raeford, Andrew Reed, Robert Tarpey, Doug Tate, Butch, Vann and Skip Warren, and Gary "Gee Whiz" Jones.

I would also like to express my deep appreciation to my publisher, editor, and friend, Rollin Riggs.

Very special thanks are also due to John and Penny Lind, their son Gabby and daughter Polly, plus Mike Murphy and Chuck Rose for their hospitality and thoughtfulness in providing me with a wonderful little cabin up in the woods where I lived while finishing the manuscript, and to my friend James for turning me on to them.

Also extra, extra special thanks to my dear friend Robin Crozer, who aided me immeasurably by typing my manuscript and preparing it for publication.

I couldn't have done it without ya!

Bill Barnes

Preface

IN 1984, A close friend got a phone call from a buddy named (believe it or not) Mike Missile, who was organizing a team of rookies to play the latest craze sweeping southern California, The Survival Game®. My friend had to decline, but he told Mike to call me.

Frankly, I thought the idea of getting all dressed up in camouflage clothing and running around the woods shooting my fellow humans with paint pellets had to be about the coolest thing I'd ever heard of in my life! And when Mike asked me if I knew anybody else who might be interested, my friend Tony Mederos immediately came to mind.

So I called Tony, and he was as thrilled at the prospect as I was. A few weeks later we had our first taste of this exciting new game. We were hooked.

Although we got "educated" by experienced players who knew how to play as a team, we still had a blast. In the third game that day, I employed my very first "banzai charge" and managed to eliminate three opponents, and I was looking

for a fourth when I finally got zapped. That game alone left me with an adrenaline rush that lasted for days!

I captained my own team for a few months until Mike Keyes talked Bill Saugez and me into joining his group, the No Name Team. (We liked to remain *very* anonymous!) Under his leadership, we won the National Survival Game's Western Regional Championship and then played in the 1985 Nationals in Houston.

Later, I played with the Navarones, a two-team grouping known individually as Navarone Armageddon and Navarone Apocalypse. Under the inspired leadership of Andy Greenwell and Jim Daniels, these two teams achieved some remarkable victories. Navarone Armageddon took first place in the 1987 New York Open (at the time, the largest paintball tournament ever), while "maxing out" (i.e., obtaining perfect scores) in every game they played. And Navarone Apocalypse took second place in the 1987 NSG North American Championships in Pittsburgh, while going undefeated for the tournament.

So you might say that I've had a little experience playing with high caliber teams!

As I played with all these teams, I gained considerable experience and skill as a player. I was also able to observe the strengths and weaknesses of both my opponents and my teammates.

One day, at a post-game pizza and beer gathering with Tony and Peter Wrenn, we came to realize how much we had learned over the past few years. During the game that day, we had observed our novice friends make many of the same mistakes we used to make. Thus, the idea for this book was born.

I started thinking back to how scared and nervous I had been during my first game, and I knew that the main reason was my almost total lack of knowledge of how to actually *play* the game! How, exactly, should I respond when I encountered the enemy? Should I stay with a group, or try to be Rambo? I had no idea.

Then, after I'd played a few times and knew the rudiments of the game, I realized I knew *nothing* about strategy and tactics. Oh, I could fire my gun and sometimes even hit people, but I had no finesse, no style—and no plan. And I had no idea how to organize and motivate my teammates.

Well, I know a lot about paintball now, and it's my sincere hope that this book will prepare you for your first games and then help you develop into a skillful, cunning player much quicker than the trial-and-error method I had to use. Of course, there's no substitute for actual game experience, so get out there and play as much as you can.

I hope this book will prove useful to you in your endeavor to become a superior player. Good luck and, above all, have fun!

Contents

Beyond Capture the Flag:

Introduction

SINCE YOU'VE EXPRESSED enough interest to acquire this book, you've probably had some exposure to paintball (also known as the Survival Game®, "air gun games," "Capture the Flag for Adults," etc.). Even if you haven't played yet, you've probably heard about it from your friends or the media. On the other hand, you may be a veteran of many "firefights," and now you're looking for ways to improve your skills.

Regardless of your prior experience, you've come to the right place. First, this book will help novice players quickly understand the game, what to do in basic game situations, and what their teammates expect from them. But intermediate and advanced players will benefit most from this book. Ideas for motivating and organizing your team, strategies for dealing with various terrains, tactics for defeating enemy plans—all are addressed herein. Plus, we've described a number of fascinating "scenarios"—unique ways to play paintball other than the standard "Capture the Flag" version. Throughout, we've included diagrams and drawings that will help you clearly understand the tactical concepts discussed in the text.

In short, this book should help all paintball players play the game better and have even more fun on the field.

★★★★★★★★★

First, a brief history and explanation of the sport is in order.

The original game was the brainchild of three men: Charles Gaines, the author of *Pumping Iron*; Hayes Noel, a New York City stockbroker; and Robert Gurnsey, who owned a ski shop at the time. These three had been arguing among themselves about the origin of a person's ability to survive. Was it an instinctual trait, or was it a learned response? Could a city boy survive as well in a rural setting as a country boy, for example? And how would a country boy make out in an "urban jungle?"

Their debate continued for several years. Then, one of the men happened to see an ad in a farm catalog for a cattle-marking pistol. They realized they had found the key ingredient to stage a contest that would settle their argument—a very symbolic instrument of punishment for making the wrong move in a "survival" situation.

The first paintball game was played in June of 1981 near Henniker, New Hampshire. There were 12 participants— the three originators and nine of their friends—and they played what is now known as the "individual" version of the game. Each player started at a different location on the 100-acre playing field and tried to collect a flag from each of four flag stations located around the field. The first player who accomplished this (while avoiding being shot by the others) and left the field with the four flags in hand would win. It was strictly every man for himself.

The winner of the first game was a New Hampshire forester named Ritchie White. He won by sheer stealth. He was never seen by any other players during the entire game, and he never fired a shot.

It seems that everyone involved, however, had one hell of a good time, and the rest, as they say, is history. The game started getting a huge amount of publicity, with articles appearing in *Time* and *People* magazines, among others. The more people heard about it, the more they wanted to play. In response, the game's inventors formed a corporation, National Survival Game, Inc. of New London, New Hampshire, to establish dealerships and create products for the game.

Paintball Today

These days, the individual version is not played very often, and the team version of the game—basically a twist on the old kids' game "Capture the Flag"—is far more popular.

In the team version, two teams square-off at opposite ends of the field. The fields, although of various sizes and dimensions, are almost never anywhere near as large as the 100-acre field on which the first game was played. Ten or 20 acres is a much more common size for present-day game fields.

For officially sanctioned games, teams are limited to 15 players each, but the number can vary widely for "fun games" —sometimes up to 40 or 50 players on a side. Some "Weekend Wars" in southern California have even featured teams of over 500 people per side, with various embellishments like "medics," troop movements via helicopter, and "strafing runs" by ultralights dropping paint pellets!

Each team wears a different colored armband for identification purposes and tries to capture its opponents' flag while preventing the capture of its own. In the team game, pitched battles, or "firefights," between members of the two sides are common, as the teams try to gain ground toward each others' flag. If one team can secure its opponents' flag and return it safely to its home flag station, it wins the game. If the time limit (usually 45 minutes or one hour) expires before either team can accomplish this, then the team that has inflicted heavier losses on its enemy wins.

Casualties occur whenever a player is marked with a certain quantity of paint. He or she is then considered "dead" for that game and must immediately leave the field without talking.

Players are marked, and thereby eliminated, with small (.68 caliber, to be exact), round, gelatin capsules filled with water-soluble paint. They usually shatter on impact, leaving a bright "splat" of paint. When fired from close to medium range, they can sting a little, but seldom bad enough to break the skin or even leave a welt. Since the pellets could cause serious eye injuries, players must wear safety goggles at all times during the game. A player who removes his goggles on the field is almost always "out" immediately.

The pellets are fired from various models of airguns, all of which are powered by carbon dioxide (CO_2) charges. Most guns are reasonably accurate to about 100 feet, although they can shoot much farther.

Players usually wear camouflage clothing, although first-time players often just wear old jeans and a dark t-shirt. Many players go all out and cover their exposed skin with camouflage paint and even put leaves and branches in their hair. Goggles with full face masks are increasingly popular, especially among players who have been hit by a paint pellet in the mouth. The red pellets, for example, are not cherry-flavored!

The fields are usually run by entrepreneurs who provide a playing field(s), rental guns, and referees for the action for a fee ranging from $20 to $50 per player for the day. Players usually will have to purchase extra ammo (paint pellets and CO_2 cartridges) and maybe lunch during the day, so the total cost for the day's outing is about $30 to $70.

If a person wants to play but doesn't know anyone with a team, he can contact the field operators, who will gladly fix him up with a team captain looking for players. Many fields have "walk-on days," where everyone is simply divided up at random into two groups for the day.

Who Plays Paintball?

All types of people play paintball regularly, but they're mostly (perhaps contrary to what you might have envisioned) pretty non-radical folks. Though they might adopt a warrior's facade during the game, paintball players are no more belligerent or aggressive, on average, than the members of the typical bowling league or softball team. They might actually be even less rowdy, since paintball gives them a great outlet to release pent-up hostilities.

Furthermore, although the trademarked version of the game is called The Survival Game® , it generally doesn't appeal much to people known as "survivalists," who usually believe that a nuclear or racial conflict is imminent and who plan to stay alive during and after the "war." Since paintball is long on fantasy and short on realism—and played far too much in the spirit of jest—it's usually not attractive to people interested in preparing for true survival situations.

In fact, the game is definitely a poor training ground for real combat. Because of the gun-play involved in the sport, players might learn something about surviving a shoot-out, but the game's foremost purpose is very innocent: to have fun. And its foremost concerns—running around in the woods, playing hide-and-seek, and trying to shoot your buddies with paint—are harmless and a real kick! No more, no less.

The folks at National Survival Game headquarters estimate that nearly 100,000 people play the game every weekend—and that's just in the U.S.! Thousands more play on fields all over the world—Canada, Europe, Australia, South Africa, Asia. One equipment company, Crossfire, Inc., has estimated that over six million people have played the game in the United States to date. In southern California—a real hotbed of paintball enthusiasm—there are over 50 different game fields and at least 15 retail stores catering solely to paintballers. These stores sell all the equipment necessary to play the game at one stop, rather than having to truck all over town from army surplus stores, to sporting goods stores, to gun stores—as players used to do.

In addition, there's a slick, national magazine devoted to the sport: *Action Pursuit Games*, considered the industry's leading journal. The magazine publishes game results, news on upcoming tournaments and events, and tips on how to play the game better, plus product reviews and ads for the fields, gear and specialty shops.

The way interest in the sport has exploded has been simply phenomenal, and it's estimated that the game won't peak in popularity for many years, since there are so many people who have not yet played and so many new scenarios to add excitement to the game. The sport has blossomed so quickly, in fact, and generated so much media attention, that many people have called it "The Sport of the 90's."

Paintball's Allure

And why are all these people so thrilled over this silly activity?

Because, as an ad for a southern California field called Sat Cong Village once said, it offers "a sense of adventure the protected will never know." Paintball offers an adrenaline-releasing entertainment that's—let's face it—simply not found in bowling or golf. It provides a unique opportunity to taste "the thrill of victory and the agony of defeat" in a more profound tableau than other team sports.

Also, the sense of camaraderie that usually occurs among teammates in any sport tends to be magnified in paintball, due to the mock-dangerous nature of the game. Paintball, therefore, has a built-in tendency to promote an enjoyable sense of togetherness among participants.

In fact, this bonding element can be a beneficial side-effect of paintball participation. Many large corporations have taken advantage of this facet of play—Rockwell International, McDonnell Douglas, Hughes Aircraft, Marriott Hotels, Sears, etc.—and have fielded teams to boost the morale of their employees. Disneyland employees even formed two teams: Danbos' Commandos and, believe it or not, Mickey's Jihad!

Besides the feelings of kinship with your teammates, players often experience a post-game sense of release, a feeling of well-being, an exorcism of the tensions and anxieties of everyday life. The game is definitely very intense and, while playing, participants usually experience a thrilling sense of heightened awareness, a deepening of perception, and a feeling of being "really alive." These feelings come from the game's illusion of danger. Many people also enjoy the chance to shed their polite, everyday, "civilian" image and play "Sgt. Rock" or "Rambo" for a day, without anyone getting hurt.

But, more than anything else, it's the sheer, exhilarating fun of the sport that has been responsible for its amazingly rapid growth during the past few years. It has a delightful capacity to make you forget your grown-up worries and become just like a rambunctious kid again. And this is perhaps the most wonderful aspect of the whole paintball experience.

For all these reasons, a large percentage of people who try the game quickly become "hooked" and return to play weekend after weekend. Regardless of how often or why you play, I've written this book to help you improve as a player and to increase your level of skill and confidence more quickly. So, read the text that follows, absorb all the knowledge from it you can, and then get out there and have fun!

The Rules of the Game

I N MY EXPERIENCE, opportunities to play the individual variation of paintball range from rare to nonexistent. The most popular and widely played version is the team game, so that is what this book will focus on.

While many fields employ different variations and scenarios, in this text we will concentrate on the standard, Capture the Flag version of the game. And usually, unless otherwise specified, we will be dealing with the single-flag version, as opposed to the double-flag version, of the game. Of course, the vast majority of the advice herein will apply to most any situation you'll encounter in paintball.

The object of the game in single-flag Capture the Flag is very simple:

Capture your opponent's flag and return it to your flag station before your opponent gets your flag to his flag station.

At the beginning of the game, each team starts at oppo-

site ends of the field at its home flag station. Two judges, in either radio or verbal contact, will conduct a simultaneous countdown to start the action. The field should have well-defined boundaries, and the game should have a time limit. One hour games are most common. Unless they choose to play a strictly defensive game, each team will try to steal the enemy flag and return it safely to its home base.

If neither team can accomplish this during the specified time limit, the judges will take a body-count to determine the winner—that is, the team with the most "kills" wins, unless one or both teams have flag captures, which usually earn bonus points. Therefore, if one team has suffered more casualties than the other but has one or more flag captures to its credit, it might win the game on the basis of a greater overall point total.

Of course, paintball games are also largely games of elimination. An **elimination** occurs when a player is marked with a certain quantity of paint. A common rule-of-thumb on many fields is that you must be marked with a splat of paint about the size of a quarter to be eliminated. Some fields allow a splat only the size of a dime, and some consider only "direct hits" as eliminations—regardless of the amount of paint present. On some fields, "head shots" (hits above the collarbone) don't count; other fields say any hit anywhere means you're "dead."

When in doubt, players may call for a **paint check**, which is a time-out to determine whether an elimination has, in fact, occurred. Often, a player will feel a hit on his back or some other unviewable area and will have no way of knowing if the pellet actually broke. This is what paint checks are for.

If the player in question is unmarked, the game will resume. If, however, he does indeed show a quantity of paint sufficient for elimination, he immediately announces the fact, puts on an **elimination vest**, and leaves the field by the most direct route available. He should *not* remove his goggles until he's well off the field.

Dead men do not talk! The only permissible utterances are "Dead man coming through" or "I'm dead! Don't shoot!" or similar phrases. But an eliminated player may not give his name or any information to his teammates in any manner whatsoever—either by word or gesture. If a dead man gives information to a teammate, the teammate is also eliminated. This tends to make teammates very angry! Therefore, it's wise to observe this rule strictly.

Scoring differs widely from field to field, but players will almost always have a point value. Also, bonus points are usually awarded for successful flag captures, even if the flag is not successfully returned. At some fields, only the first flag capture earns bonus points. A **flag capture** is defined as a player pulling the flag from the enemy flag pole without being marked by enemy pellets. Even if he gets only two steps with the flag before being shot, he would still be credited with a successful capture, as long as he was clean when the flag was pulled. Since a successful flag capture is often worth many more points than an individual player, it's sometimes worth sacrificing yourself if you're near the flag.

The current system of scoring in officially sanctioned National Survival Game contests is based on a total possible score of 145 points per game. In these contests, each of the 15 players is worth three points, the first flag capture is worth 20, and a successful flag return is worth 80. This is a good system, as capturing the flag becomes both teams' paramount objective. Hence, very aggressive play is both promoted and rewarded.

Once a player has captured the enemies' flag, he acquires a special status. He becomes a **flag carrier**. If the flag carrier is shot while trying to return the flag, two things might happen, depending on the rules of the field:

The most common rule is that, upon his elimination, the flag carrier becomes a roving flag station. He must announce the fact that he is hit, put on his elimination vest, and then walk in a straight line back to the enemy flag station, where he must return the stolen flag to its original position. He must then leave the field, all the while observing the rules pertaining to dead players.

However, since he is considered a roving flag station, any player, whether friend or foe, may grab the flag from him. (The flag carrier may not hand or throw the flag to another player or announce the fact that he has it.) The flag must be visible at all times during its journey across the field. Of course, it's in the best interest of the dead flag carrier's teammates to recover the flag from him and continue to take it to their home base. Therefore, it's wise for the flag carrier to have at least one teammate by his side at all times to serve as an "escort." This escort can grab the flag from the flag carrier in the event he gets hit.

Another variant that's gaining popularity is exactly the same as above, except that the eliminated flag carrier simply stands where he got hit and holds the flag out for whichever player gets there first.

A less common variation, in which protection of the flag carrier becomes even more crucial, is when no one may take the flag from an eliminated flag carrier, who must return the flag to the enemy flag station personally.

In single-flag paintball, a team wins when it gets the enemy flag to its home flag station. If the judge declares the flag carrier free of marks, the game is over.

In double-flag paintball, the game is over only when one team has both flags secured at its home flag station—its flag, and its opponent's. In this version, a team may successfully capture the enemy flags, but if its own flag has been captured in the meantime, the game continues until one team has both flags securely hung at its home flag station or until time expires.

Although rules may vary slightly from field to field, these are the basic rules of paintball. In the following chapters, we will examine more fully many of these rules and concepts, as well as offer alternatives to the basic game.

Paintball Equipment

THE MOST IMPORTANT piece of equipment in a paintball game is not your gun—it's your **eye protection**! You **must** wear your goggles **at all times** while the game is in progress. And your elimination is no reason whatsoever to remove them, since you could be shot inadvertently while leaving the field. We cannot emphasize enough the importance of wearing your goggles constantly while you are on the playing field or in any area where people are firing their paintguns.

Sometimes, especially on hot days, your goggles may fog. Fogging is still **no excuse** for removing your goggles. Even if you are shot because your vision was impaired by fogged goggles, at least you'll be able to view the world with both eyes when you leave the field!

Paintball is played with airguns that hurl a brittle gelatin capsule at a muzzle velocity of anywhere from 240 to 340 feet per second—about ⅓ the velocity of many handgun cartridges. You don't want to get hit in the eye with a paint pellet!

The field will supply goggles, or you may bring your own.

Most dedicated players own their own goggles, since those supplied by the fields are often scratched.

If you purchase your own eye protection, choose goggles that *completely surround* your eye area, and test them for sturdiness by shooting them several times at point-blank range (off your face, of course!). If possible, use a weapon that fires at or near the maximum allowable muzzle velocity for the field you'll be playing on. Uvex PC-4C is one model I know that can definitely withstand the rigors of paintball competition.

You should also be sure to clean your goggles thoroughly—with water only—immediately after use. Paint, if left in extended contact with many plastic lenses, can cause a dangerous deterioration of the material.

When playing on fields that are shady, I prefer amber lenses, as they "lighten up" your vision by about 20%. This gives you sort of a "cat's eyes" effect, letting you see (and, you hope, pick-off) enemies lurking in the shadows.

Glare is a common problem. When they look toward the sun, players can be nearly blind. Needless to say, when this happens, you are at a big disadvantage vis-á-vis your enemy. And to make matters worse, not only will you be unable to spot your enemies, but they can easily see you from the reflection off your goggles! Clear goggles are the worst for glare, and the amber types are prone to glare also. A camouflage baseball cap to shade your eyes is one easy solution to this problem.

For the more open, sunny fields, dark green goggles are the choice of many players. They will never glare, plus there's no white plastic reflection to give away your position.

Clothes & Masks

Most people prefer to wear clothes marked with a camouflage pattern ("cammies") when they play paintball, though it's perfectly fine to wear an old pair of jeans and a dark shirt, if you prefer. There are many different patterns of camouflage available. The three most common types are jungle ("tiger stripes"), woodland, and desert (see illustration). The desert type, a tan and brown configuration, is inappropriate for fields with heavy foliage. Jungle and woodland camouflage, both configurations of green, black, and brown, are pretty much interchangeable. The jungle pattern, made famous by the U. S. Special Forces in Southeast Asia, is appropriate for shadier fields with a lot of thick cover. Woodland cammies are a little bit more suitable on sunny, open fields that still have a lot of green foliage.

Many rookie players over-emphasize the value of camou-

Jungle pattern (tiger stripes)

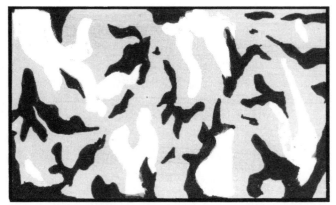

Woodland pattern

Desert pattern

flage. While it can be quite useful, especially in ambush situations, it has limited value once you've been spotted and
a firefight is underway. While it certainly won't hurt to cover
yourself completely with camo paint—it's a good way to "get
psyched" before the game—seasoned players don't waste
much time on elaborate camouflage. They know that elements like courage and cunning will have much more impact on the outcome of a game.

Regardless of which pattern of camouflage is most appropriate on the fields where you play, you'll want to choose
outfits with as many pockets as possible to stash your supplies. Pants should have at least six pockets (the standard
four, plus two more on the thighs), and shirts should have
at least four. And remember: carry only one metal item per
pocket. Otherwise, they'll clang together and give away your
position!

In addition to your elimination vest, spare pellets, and extra CO_2 cartridges, you might want to carry the following:
a bandana, a small bottle of defogger, tissue paper (for cleaning splatters from your goggles), a short piece of shotgun
swab for cleaning your gun barrel, and insect repellant if
bugs are a problem. And if you really hate being eliminated, you might bring some cash with you to try to bribe the
enemy!

Baseball caps, floppy "boonie hats," or hunter-type hats
will all provide you with a bit of shade and therefore protect from glare. Berets are fine, too, as long as the field is
shady or you have non-reflective lenses in your goggles.

As for footgear, regular tennis shoes, especially the kind
with velcro straps, are fine if they are a dark color and there's
no water on the field. If, however, there's a stream or shallow river that you must cross frequently, you might want to
acquire a pair of vented combat boots, which allow water
to drain quickly. Tennis shoes tend to get too soggy if you
run through water.

Another good choice, especially to add a degree of safety

on muddy days, are athletic shoes with cleats, like those for soccer and football.

The main thing to look for in your footwear is weight. The lighter the better! Paintball games can be strenuous affairs, and by the third or fourth game your legs will be exhausted if you wear heavy footgear.

Many players also wear gloves. Ordinary brown cloth gardeners' gloves with the fingers cut out are my personal favorites. If nothing else, they're good for giving you a macho image!

Although the rules of the game disallow any type of general body padding, I've never known any fields that objected to knee pads or elbow pads, or to padded bras for women.

Sweatbands, either on the head or the wrists, are also popular with many players. Wearing a sweatband or bandana on your head will help prevent goggle fogging.

Also, a belt is a mandatory item of clothing, and not just to hold your pants up! Belts are useful to hold pouches that carry your supplies in a handy position. There are pouches specially designed to hold paint tubes and/or CO_2, and they can be quite useful.

A watch is another important item, since the amount of time remaining in a game can be a critical factor as you are deciding on the best course of action.

I also highly recommend a face mask made of hard plastic, like a hockey goalie's mask, although usually not as stout. These wonderful devices can save you fat lips and unsightly welts on your face, and they give you an invaluable sense of confidence in close shoot-out situations. If you ever use the "banzai" technique described later in this book, a face mask is essential.

A face mask also keeps your goggles a little bit off your face, thereby increasing air circulation and alleviating the fogging problem. Usually fogging will not be a problem, even on the hottest days, if you wear a face mask and also clean your lenses with a defogger/cleaner solution. Always remove

Navarone Bill Homa models the excellent facemask/goggle from J.T. Paintball.

the solution with tissue paper—paper towels tend to scratch. Some high-tech goggles even have miniature fans built-in to cool your face and further discourage fogging.

Many manufacturers have created face protection that combines a face mask and goggles in one unit. Having the two built as one piece of equipment is a great idea, as it adds an extra element of safety by eliminating the possibility of your goggles becoming slightly misaligned with your face mask and thereby leaving open a small, but dangerous, gap where paint and gelatin fragments could penetrate. A company called J. T. Paintball makes one of the best goggle/face mask units that I've seen. Built especially for paintball, it's been tested to withstand the impact of high-velocity paint pellets, and the goggles are a special anti-fog type.

Paintball Guns

Now for the section you've all been waiting for—the guns!

The original paintball gun is the Nel-Spot 007, a CO_2-operated, bolt-action pistol created to mark cattle and trees. Despite its humble beginnings, the Nel-Spot is still my personal favorite. The addition of a pump on the Nel-Spot is a great improvement over the old bolt-action mechanism, which is rather awkward to operate.

The Sheridan is another gun that vies with the Nel-Spot as the favorite of paintballers. Some players claim it has greater accuracy than the Nel-Spot. I think it's harder to change CO_2 in the Sheridan and harder to reload paint pellets if it isn't equipped with a speed-loader. But many players swear by it.

Another popular weapon is a cute, submachine-gun-looking thing called an "Uzi." Like the previous guns, it uses a gravity-feed mechanism to chamber the rounds. One advantage is its large magazine capacity: 38 rounds. They do take some getting used to, however, as they tend to shoot high. Players often just point these guns, sometimes firing from the hip, rather than actually aiming them.

In general, I would advise you to avoid revolver-type paintguns, since they are usually painfully slow to reload and tend to burst pellets. They just aren't machined accurately enough to obtain the exact alignment of cylinder and barrel necessary to fire something as fragile as a paint pellet.

The Splatmaster Rapide, the second generation of the widely-used gun from National Survival Game, Inc., has quickly gained popularity. The Rapide is a semi-automatic that holds either 20 or 40 pellets, and it's quite reasonably priced. NSG also offers an upgraded version of the Rapide called the Comp, with a forward grip, back stock, and constant air.

Besides the four weapons mentioned, many other paintguns are available, including a fully-automatic, clip-fed model called the SMG-60. Some of the newer guns are excellent, some mediocre, and a few, frankly, stink. For the latest guns, I recommend you compare ads and reviews in magazines like *Action Pursuit Games* and then conduct extensive test-firing yourself—before you part with your bucks. *Caveat emptor.*

With the explosion in paintball's popularity, many accessories and modifications have been developed for paintguns. In my opinion, the most useful accessory is a device called a speed-loader. They come in many different styles and configurations, but their purpose is simple: they allow you to avoid replacing the plastic tube each time you reload. A speed-loader is a tube of a diameter sufficient to accommodate paint pellets, the far end of which has a flexible device that allows you to insert a fresh tube of paint, load the pellets, and then withdraw the empty tube. The device then springs back into place, thereby preventing the pellets from falling out. Some speed-loaders are very long to hold many pellets; others are designed with an upward slant, giving a constant "gravity feed" so you don't have to tilt your gun down before chambering a fresh round.

Such things as scopes, shoulder stocks, and barrel extenders (which *do* increase accuracy substantially, by the way) are also available. Even "silencers" have become common! Some fields allow these modifications, and some don't.

A rather controversial item on the paintball scene is the attachment, via a hose, of a tank of CO_2 to your weapon. It's called "constant air." Although I have a few reservations about this particular modification (which I will address more fully in a later chapter), constant air can be useful from a practical standpoint, as it allows a player to fire without worrying about changing CO_2 or running low during a firefight. It also has the major advantage of greatly increasing accuracy, since each shot is propelled with almost exactly the same amount of air pressure as the next, rather than with the decreasing charge of air that occurs with the standard CO_2 cartridges (which are usually good for only 15-20 shots each).

Weapons with constant air are quite common, though many fields ban the use of "CA." I prefer a more spartan approach and, like the majority of players on the Navarone team, I rely on the use of stock weapons without constant air. Playing without it develops more skill and finesse in your game. And if you're interested in serious competition, it's not a good idea to become used to playing with constant air, because it's not allowed in many tournaments.

Recently, many players have been enlarging the valve stems of their guns to admit a larger amount of CO_2, thereby increasing the muzzle velocity of the weapons. This can be a potentially dangerous practice. Fortunately, all reputable fields have chronographs, which they require players who bring their own weapons to shoot through before the games. Typically, any gun shooting over 300 feet per second is disallowed. The obvious danger in allowing guns that shoot harder is that players could be wearing goggles that might not withstand the impact of "magnum pellets." Plus, the pellets generally hurt just enough to make the game interesting as it is, and it would be unfair and downright mean to increase their velocity any further!

TACTICAL TIP #1

Always carry your equipment in the same places or pockets every time you play. That way, you'll always know exactly where everything is, and you won't have to fumble for something in the heat of battle.

Conditioning

WHILE YOU CERTAINLY don't have to be in peak shape to be an effective paintball player, the sport *is* strenuous, and being physically fit definitely can give you an edge.

In general, offense is much more physically demanding than defense. After all, offensive players must quickly traverse the length of the field *twice* during a successful flag assault. Defensive players, however, probably will run only a few yards during a game, unless they need to recapture a stolen flag. (A "forward defense," such as Bill Saugez and I used to play, is more strenuous.)

Therefore, when dividing up your team, you should usually assign the "Old and Slow" to defense and the "Young and Fast" to your assault group.

Since paintball is not a contact sport, strength training has no real application—unless, of course, you become so muscular that just the *sight* of you intimidates your opponents!

Besides contributing to your general good health, any aer-

obic exercise will serve you well in building the speed and stamina necessary to become a superior assault player. Sports that require strenuous, sustained exertion such as judo, soccer, swimming, or track would be good, complementary activities for you if you are serious about becoming an outstanding paintball player.

A good player is always alert and calculating, and being physically fit will benefit your mind as well. You'll be able to think more clearly and rationally if you're not out of breath and your heart isn't pounding out of your chest. And don't forget—heavy breathing can give away your location!

Remember also that paintball frequently requires quick reactions: you often have to whirl around to fire or suddenly dive for cover. If you haven't warmed up before the game, such hasty maneuvers can lead to injuries like pulled and sprained muscles. *Always* take a few minutes before the game to do a few stretching exercises. Stretching out, along with a few calisthenics, will save you some soreness and injury and get your blood pumping, making you more mentally alert. While your buddies are wasting their time putting camo paint all over their face, you'll be doing something truly beneficial by getting your muscles and your mind ready for the game.

After all, paintball, like most things in life, is largely mind over matter. Get the blood pumping, get the adrenaline flowing, and you'll be amazed at how well you play.

Now that we've covered the preliminaries, let's proceed to a discussion of some basic elements of play...

Two Crucial Concepts:
Fields of Fire and *Flanking*

Fields of Fire

The field of fire, a crucial concept for the paintball player to understand, is simply the area where you may fire your weapon relatively unobstructed. In other words, it's the area of the field that you can *command* with your firepower.

Page 40 illustrates the concept:

Assume that the areas between the patches of cover consist of open spaces with minimal obstacles. The arrows indicate the areas where Player A can shoot relatively unobstructed—his **field of fire**. In this position, Player A—protected against ambush from behind and the sides by the thicket—can command a field of fire of almost 180-degrees. He is in a very good defensive position.

Of course, in actual games, the areas of cover and the open spaces won't be so well-defined, but the illustration serves as a graphic depiction of the concept. And it's a concept that all accomplished paintball players are constantly con-

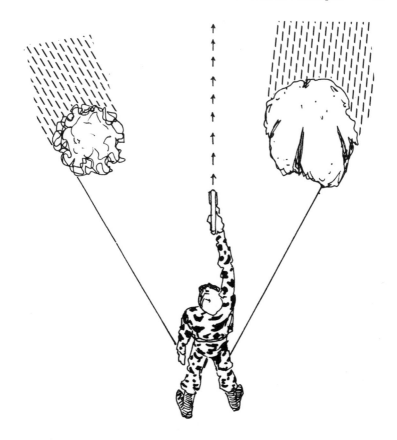

sidering, if only subconsciously. In any confrontation, if you (or you and your teammates) can maneuver to command a greater total field of fire than the enemy's total field of fire, you will greatly increase your odds of winning the firefight.

Consider the illustration again. If player A were a defensive player, he would probably want to hold his position, since it's a strong one. Let's assume, however, that Player A is an *offensive* player, advancing toward the enemy flag. Assume further that, upon acquiring his position at the edge of the patch of thick cover, he has surveyed the surrounding area without spotting any opponents. He has heard some movement in the opposite thicket, however, and is highly suspi-

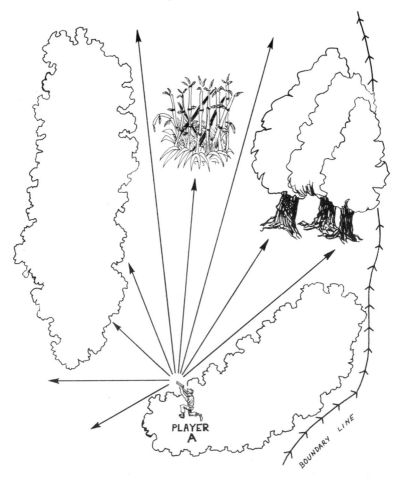

PLAYER
A

BOUNDARY LINE

cious of it. He is sure, though, that the tree area is safe, and he knows that Player B has scouted the eastern end of his thicket and declared it safe.

Question: What route should Player A take to advance downfield? The next illustration diagrams his safest path.

Player A carefully skirts the edge of the thicket, keeping inside the cover just enough to be protected from possible enemy fire, but close enough to the edge to maintain visual surveillance of the suspected enemy location. Then, upon

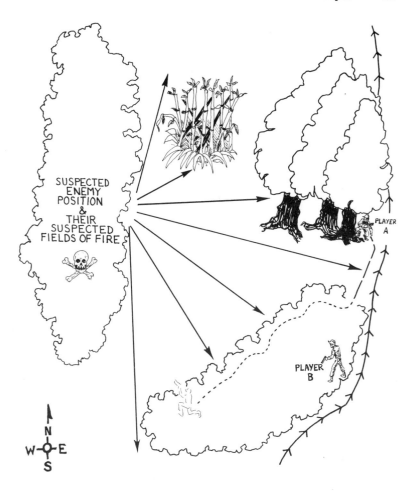

gaining the portion of the thicket closest to the next available cover (that is, the group of trees), he sprints (or perhaps crawls, depending on the circumstances) across the short vulnerable area.

In the illustration, Player A advanced in such a way as to *minimize* his exposure to the enemy's field of fire. Enemies lurking anywhere in the opposite thicket would have, at best, a very limited field of fire against Player A—15-degrees or less. And once he has safely crossed the gap between the thicket and the trees, the bamboo stand will protect him from enemy fire from the thicket. By utilizing the available cover, then crossing at the shortest possible vulnerable area, Player A has chosen a much safer path than simply breaking cover at his original position and "making a run for it" across the open ground.

This is the other side of the coin to the field of fire concept, and it tends to be especially important to members of an "assault group" —

Always advance in a manner that reduces the enemy's fields of fire against you.

Exposing themselves needlessly to enemy fire is one of the most common errors committed by rookies. As you gain experience, however, the safest moves will become almost instinctual.

We will discuss fields of fire as it relates to defensive players more fully in a later chapter. For now, suffice to say that it is crucial for you and your teammates to station yourselves in such a way that, collectively, you command the greatest possible field of fire.

TACTICAL TIP #2

Windy days favor aggressive teams. Strong gusts of wind can mask the sounds of assaulters moving through the woods, thereby negating the advantage that defenders usually enjoy of being able to hear the enemy approaching.

Flanking

"Don't worry about protecting your flanks. Let the enemy worry about protecting his." —General George S. Patton

Aside from knowing how to shoot your gun, flanking is the most important thing for paintball players to understand. Simply put, flanking is the art of two or more players "moving on" the enemy in an effort to catch him in a crossfire. Failure to employ proper flanking techniques is one of the most common shortcomings of rookies. Let's look at an example:

In the illustration on page 44, we see two groups of players of two members each. In this simplified example, we will assume the players are rookies. Both groups have taken similar positions, with one element from each group sniping at the enemy from either side of a bush. Obviously, neither group has a clear advantage, and the firefight probably will

be decided by luck—whichever group can get the "lucky" shots will win.

Now let's consider the same example, with a difference. This time, the "A" group consists of two experienced players who prefer to make their own luck.

As you can see on page 46, Player A1 disengages and goes around the bush to whisper to A2, "Keep the guy on the right [Player B2] pinned down—I'm going to flank him." Assume that Player B1 is inexperienced and, instead of attempting a counter-flank, he holds his position when Player A1 disengages, thereby effectively neutralizing himself. This may seem unlikely but, believe me, rookies commit this error all the time.

As Player A2 fires round after round of suppressive fire at B2—so rapidly that B2 has almost no chance to return fire—Player A1 quickly sprints from cover to cover until he has attained the position indicated.

Since Player B2 has left his side exposed, A2 is able to eliminate him quickly. Now that the "A Team" has a two-to-one advantage, they can, with proper care, finish off Player B1—almost at their leisure. This is done in the next illustration (page 47), as we extend the diagram downfield a little bit.

Player A1 continues his flanking maneuver, going around two more areas of cover while almost totally avoiding B1's field of fire. He then comes in behind B1. In the meantime, since B2 has been eliminated, Player A2 has moved over to the bush originally occupied by his teammate to lay suppressive fire on B1. The "A" group has achieved an almost complete 360-degree crossfire against its opponent, who is in a rotten position, having allowed himself to be caught without a safe line of retreat.

B1 faces almost sure elimination because he *failed to move.* It's one of the most common mistakes committed by rookies, as we will discuss in the next chapter.

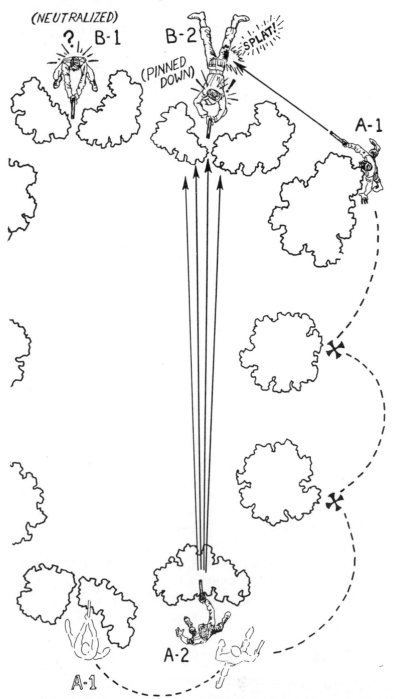

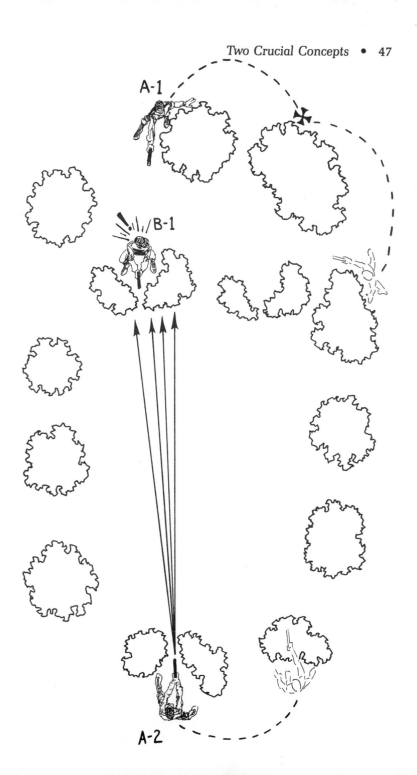

The Three Most Common Mistakes of Rookies

THE THREE most common mistakes of rookies are all sins of omission.

The first is **failure to move**. When under fire, novice players too often hold their positions and try to hide better. Experienced players know that it's almost always better to either attack or retreat rather than remain stationary and let your enemy outflank you and pick you off.

The second error is **failure to talk**. Again, in a firefight situation, an amazing number of beginners will suddenly become mute. They must think that if they don't talk, they'll become invisible! But once the enemy knows your position, silence won't do you or your team any good. Talk it up! Communication between teammates is an essential element of coordinated action.

The third common mistake is **failure to fire**. As you gain more experience, you will realize that firing can accomplish more than just eliminating the enemy. With practice, you will learn how to fire for suppression and intimidation.

Failure to Move

"If you want to remain in one spot, bring your tombstone with you!" —Andrew Reed, great American paintballer

I remember my very first paintball game at a field called L. A. Sho-Down. My friend Tony Mederos and I were members of a 16-man group who were, with the exception of two players, total novices. We were about to receive our "college education," as field owner Terry Hufford would later call it, at the hands of an experienced team.

Although I was doing my best to keep up a brave facade,

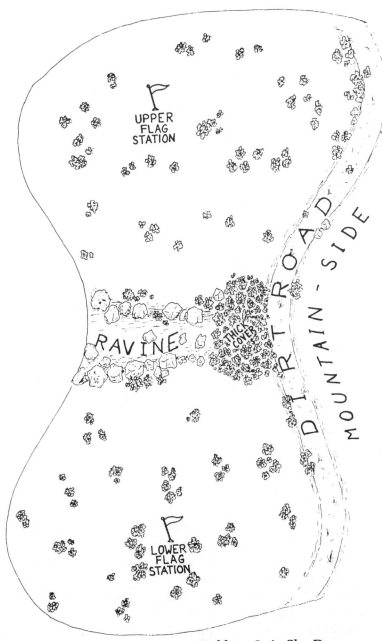

Field #1, L.A. Sho-Down

I remember a wave of anxiety as the countdown commenced. In retrospect, I realize that the main reason for my nervousness was that I had no earthly idea what I was supposed to do once I encountered the enemy! Should I charge or run or yell for help or what? I really didn't know.

Tony and I were assigned to an eight-man assault group. The whistle blew and we took off running toward the enemy flag station. Our plan wasn't totally bad—we had decided to maintain strength-in-numbers and attack as a single force, rather than split into smaller units, as many rookie teams would have done.

Our initial confrontation with the enemy, however, resulted in our total decimation and was an almost textbook example of what **not** to do in such an encounter! Our actions—or more precisely, our *inactions*—were sadly typical of a novice team.

Before I start relating our tale of woe on that fine day, I should explain the layout of the lower field at L.A. Sho-Down.

Field #1 is located at the base of a mountain, with a slight rise from one side of the field to the other. There's also has a bit of a downhill slant from the "upper" flag station to midfield. It has somewhat of an hourglass shape, with a bottleneck located halfway between the flag stations. The field narrows to maybe 75 yards at this point, the lower ⅔ of which consists of an open ravine—the "no-man's land" of this particular field. At its upper end, the ravine gives way to thick brush, and an open dirt road marks the upper boundary.

Since the field is laid out in this manner, assault groups tend to run uphill at the start of games to gain the road and then use the unobstructed pathway to advance quickly. And that is just what both asault groups decided to do on this September morning.

Our group started at the upper flag station and made the road. We were running down it when *Whack!*, our lead man was shot by an enemy ambush (see illustration). The surviving seven of us immediately ducked into the bushes.

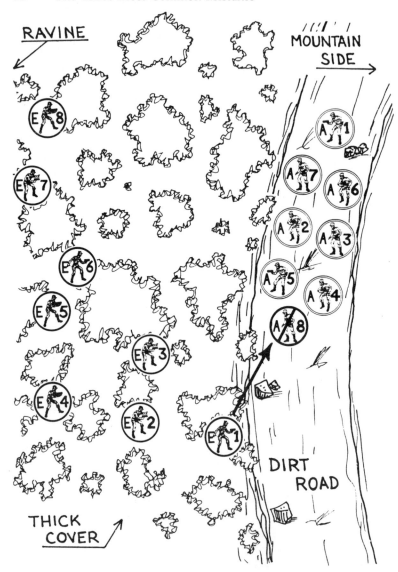

So far, besides losing a man to the ambush, we were doing O.K. But then we made our big mistake. We all just sat
there huddled in a small area, like so many startled animals
in the glare of oncoming headlights. And while we were sitting there, our experienced opponents flanked us (see illus-

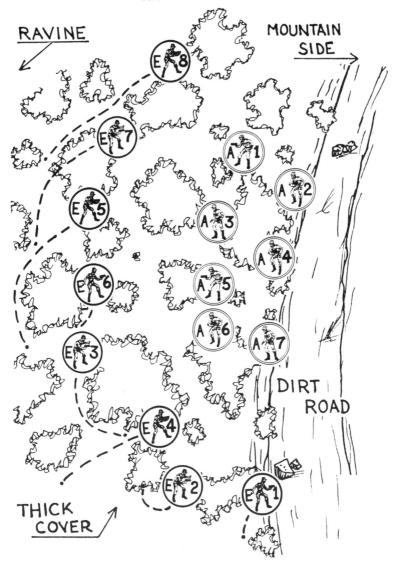

tration) and picked us off one by one. We sitting ducks quickly became dead ducks.

Our failure, like Player B2's failure from the previous chapter, was that we didn't *move*.

In paintball confrontations, it's almost always better to do something instead of nothing. Either attack, flank, or retreat, but don't just sit there!

If our team had had more experience and more confidence, we might have spread ourselves out in a manner similar to this illustration:

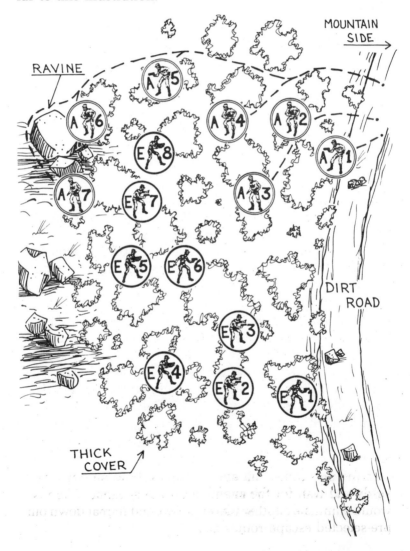

Notice how players A4 through A7 have effected a counter-flank against the enemies' initial flanking maneuver, thus preventing enemy players E5 through E8 from surrounding their positions and catching them in a crossfire, as they managed to do in the previous example.

I hope you can learn something from this little comedy of errors that my teammates and I committed the first time we played. Remember, in situations like this, do unto your enemy *before* he does unto you!

But what if you encounter an enemy group with a big numerical advantage? Well, it depends largely on the circumstances, the terrain, and the enemy's experience versus your team's experience. If your group consists of seasoned veterans and the enemy group is composed entirely of rookies, you might be able to overcome even a two-to-one disadvantage. Or, if your group is small but commands a secure defensive position, while the enemy group is large but has to cross open ground to attack you, it might be wise to hold your ground and let 'em come!

A lot depends upon the circumstances of the game and the particular mission that has been assigned to you as part of the overall team effort.

When my friend Bill Saugez and I played with the No Name Team (the 1985 National Survival Game Western Regional Champions), we were often assigned to race downfield at the start of games in the direction from which the enemy assault group would most likely attack. We usually would slow down as we approached mid-field, try to find a good ambush site with clear lines of retreat, and try to take out one or two of the enemy as they came in view. Since they didn't know it was just Bill and I, the enemy players would usually scatter into the bushes and try to assess the situation.

In the meantime, Bill and I would retreat quietly a few yards and wait for the enemy group to advance. Then we would eliminate another player or two, and retreat down our pre-selected escape routes again.

Our primary job in this instance was not to play "Rambo" and try to defeat the entire enemy assault group ourselves. Rather, it was to slow down their advance and buy time, while our assault group rapidly advanced downfield and stole the flag. We knew that if our assault group could capture the enemy flag before the enemy assault group had even seen our flag station, we would be the odds-on favorite to win that game.

We often employed various tricks, such as running from bush to bush and firing, or calling out instructions to several imaginary teammates, giving the impression of a much larger force. As I said, anything to buy time!

So remember: retreat doesn't always mean defeat. A strategic retreat, such as Bill and I used, can help a small force stay alive by harassing and confusing the enemy. Obviously, we had to keep moving to accomplish our objectives. Our efforts would have been for naught, and the two of us would have been quickly overwhelmed, had we attempted to stay in one position.

Most of what we've discussed has concerned movements of teams or groups. There is one instance where it is *imperative* that you, as an individual, move immediately: when a pellet barely misses you, and you don't know where it came from! Whether you're in a firefight or stalking through woods, you must immediately scramble for cover when an unexpected pellet smashes within inches of your position. They know where you are, and you can bet the next shot will be more accurate. Don't sit there and give the enemy a second chance!

It sounds like so much common sense, doesn't it? But I'm always amazed by the number of players who hold their exact positions when my first pellet misses them by inches, thereby giving me a second chance to zero in. If you find yourself in this situation, *always* dive for cover first, *then* take time to assess the field. Believe me, you'll see a lot more game time if you do.

Failure to Talk

The second big sin of rookie players is silence. They seem to lose their power of speech in the midst of heavy action.

Sure, there are many times in paintball where quiet and stealth are imperative. All experienced players recognize this. But, once a firefight is underway and the enemy is obviously aware of your position, talk it up! In order for your group of players to function as a team, there *must* be communication between members.

Suppose you're the "point man" of an assault group. You encounter a group of enemy players, and it's quite obvious—by the fact that pellets are splattering inches from your face—that they are aware of your presence. By all means, start shouting out any pertinent information (such as their size, location, movement, etc.) to your teammates! There's nothing for you to gain by clamming up. If your teammates' positions have not yet been revealed to the enemy, your buddies might have an advantage by remaining quiet and trying to get the first shot at an unwary enemy. But your advantage was lost the moment they spotted you.

Often, an experienced player will request information from

a novice teammate who's under fire—and receive only silence in reply. Don't be guilty of this! Communicating with your forces might help them save your neck by allowing them to outflank the guy firing on you.

If you spot a large enemy assault group coming down the hill, make your teammates aware of this—and at the top of your lungs, too! They will then be able to station themselves to thwart the enemy advance. And shout quickly! Remember, if they storm your position and eliminate you, you'll have to remain silent as you walk off the field—past your unsuspecting buddies.

Communication is also very useful when you've located an enemy and you want your teammates to make flanking maneuvers against his location. If Peter and I were working to eliminate a single opponent whom I had seen but Peter had not, our initial conversation might go something like this:

Peter (hearing my shots): "Where's he at?"

Bill: "See the oak tree? He's directly behind the first bush to our left side of it."

Peter: "O.K., got it."

Whether further conversation would ensue would depend on whether Peter needed more information. In this scenario, I would probably stop talking to Peter, hoping that my opponent would forget about him somewhat. I would rather keep him anxious about *my* presence by firing round after round of supressive fire to keep him pinned down and intimidated, while Peter flanked around behind him. Of course, I would respond to Peter if he chose to communicate with me. After all, what have I go to lose? Since my pellets are whizzing around his head, the enemy already knows my location.

The above example suggests the following rule-of-thumb:

The player who is in visual contact with the enemy should almost always talk, while his teammates may or may not,

depending on circumstances and objectives.

Talking has a definite psychological advantage as well. It projects an air of confidence to shout information in the face of enemy fire. It makes it very clear to the enemy that their presence does not worry you! And conversely, it can be very intimidating to your enemies to hear you shouting out their locations to potential flankers.

When I played with the No Name Team, we all could recognize each other's voice. Our ability to communicate was as important as our accurate shots to winning the championship. With constant communication and aggressive flanking, we often eliminated large enemy groups while suffering few, if any, casualties ourselves.

Think of it in terms of nature. What types of creatures do you think of when you're asked to name animals that are known for being very quiet? Rabbits and mice quickly come to mind. Not exactly fearsome beasts, are they?

Now, which animals are known for being loud? Lions and tigers are two obvious choices. And which animals would be most appropriate for a paintball player to emulate? Lions and tigers are perfect examples, because they are known for their stealth as well. They quietly stalk their prey and then charge with an ear-shattering roar so terrifying that it momentarily paralyzes their victims.

You should take heed of their example while playing paintball. Utilize stealth and cunning while maneuvering for position, but when the time comes to attack, be ferocious!

Failure to Fire

The third big mistake rookies make is that they don't fire enough. Though I've referred to *suppressive fire* and *intimidation fire* previously, let's discuss these concepts further.

When I first started playing paintball, if a beginner teammate asked me how many tubes of paint he should take out

on the field with him, I would answer, "Oh, maybe two extra tubes, though you might not need that much." Today, I wouldn't dare go on the field with just two spare tubes of paint (20 rounds). Now when I start a game, I usually have at least 100 spare rounds with me, and even then I sometimes run short.

Why the big change? Well, as I improved as a player, I learned that firing my weapon could do more than just eliminate the enemy. As a rookie, I didn't realize this, and I seldom took shots that weren't meant to "kill." With experience, I've learned that the primary reason for firing your gun, other than to mark your enemy, is to deliver **suppressive fire**, which we'll describe as shots that splat near the enemy without hitting him. You may get in a lucky shot now and then, but the purpose of suppressive fire is to keep your foe pinned down and unable to shoot back.

There are many opportunities to use this tactic during games. Suppose your opponent has taken cover behind a large tree. If he is greeted with a pellet smashing inches from his face everytime he tries to peer around the tree, he'll be neutralized, since he'll be unable to get off any aimed return fire at you. Plus, if you're quick and accurate enough, you might eventually mark him. Also, if two or more teammates are free to fire upon the same enemy player, the suppressive fire will be even more effective, since one teammate can be shooting while the others reload.

Of course, firing gallons of paint around the enemy becomes silly after a while. Suppressive fire is worthwhile only when combined with other tactics, like flanking. A pinned-down enemy is a prime candidate to become a victim of your teammates' aggressive maneuvers.

Remember the example on page 45, where Player A2 fires "round after round" of suppressive fire at Player B2 while Player A1 quickly flanks? That is exactly the sort of play your teammates should create when you have a foe pinned down, especially if he's lying prone (such as behind a log or small rock) or is in some sort of awkward, physically limiting position. In these situations, your teammates should be able to charge to the enemy position from the sides or behind and eliminate him before he can even turn around to aim.

Remember also that the outcome of paintball games—more than in other sports, in my opinion—is largely a matter of psychology. Those players and teams who are confident and fearless will usually triumph, and those who are fearful and intimidated will lose. And this brings us to another important reason for firing your gun: intimidation.

Intimidation fire goes hand in hand with suppressive fire. Those same rounds that neutralize an opponent physically will almost always intimidate him psychologically.

Although your opponent might be in a perfectly safe position, there is something very unnerving about the unrelenting *smack, smack, smack* of pellets so close to his position. Often, because of inexperience, anxiety, or plain old bad judgement, a player in this situation will break from his position, thereby exposing himself to your elimination shots.

Though intimidation fire is often the other side of the coin of suppressive fire, there are many instances during paintball play where it occurs as a distinct tactical entity. Suppose an enemy is not vulnerable to being pinned down. It's

often good strategy just to fire shots in his direction, just to slow down his advance and keep him worried.

Remember the story of Bill Saugez's and my job of slowing down the enemy assault group's approach? This is a good example of a situation where it was in our best interest to fire rounds for intimidation. While there was little chance of our pinning down or flanking a member of a much larger force, it was certainly possible to slow down the enemy advance by firing as many shots as possible. Remember, our job was only to slow them down, and if we could land pellets close to their positions, they usually moved much more cautiously.

Defensive players (such as Bill and I were in that example) especially should learn to use intimidation fire. Let's say you're a member of a three-man contingent defending your flag, while the rest of your team has formed a large assault group to push downfield and overwhelm the enemy flag quickly.

With such a small defense, you have to expect that any larger enemy group will be able eventually to capture your flag. In this situation, it might be good strategy for you and your teammates to forget about an ambush and start firing at the enemy from as far away as possible. Your fire might be inaccurate and unlikely to hit anyone, but it will make them approach more cautiously and hence more slowly—and that's your goal. In this scenario, don't hold your fire and let the enemy waltz within rushing distance of your flag. Make 'em work for it instead. Keep firing at them until they're a bunch of intimidated, nervous wrecks!

Finally, firing pellets can have a communications function. If a teammate wants to know the exact location of a "bogey" that you've spotted, you can always fire a pellet at the enemy position to pinpoint his location. Even if you have no chance of hitting him, "marking" him in this way is often more effective than telling your buddy, "He's over by the third tree to the left."

Paintball Psychology

PSYCHOLOGY IS A decisive factor in any sporting contest, but it's especially critical in paintball games. The very nature of paintball magnifies the psychological factors present in any sport. The more games I play, the more I realize how important the mental state of the players is to their success or failure for the day.

It all boils down to the **level of confidence** present. A highly confident team or player tends to be very successful, and vice versa. It's really just that simple. Feelings of confidence for both an individual and a team are interrelated in a sort of "feedback loop." A confident individual can inspire similar emotions in his teammates; a high-spirited team can transfer courage to an apprehensive member.

But what breeds confidence?

On a team level, confidence is largely a matter of players who are familiar and comfortable with one another and who can play together as a team. A later chapter is devoted to this concept, but for now, suffice to say that it helps greatly

for a team to be composed of players who know each other and have played together. A team must possess a cohesion, or team spirit, where there's a "one-for-all and all-for-one" feeling. I've often seen teams with this kind of camaraderie defeat larger, but more disjointed, opponents.

For obvious reasons, winning itself can be a great boost for team morale. In fact, a winning tradition often nurtures the all-important feelings of togetherness on a team. A history of successful outings together will build team spirit and encourage players to stick with the team and return for game after game, weekend after weekend. This, of course, will help the group function together as a unit more effectively, which will encourage still more wins, which will, in turn, build more team spirit. It's really a never-ending circle of cause and effect. As the old saying goes, nothing succeeds like success.

This is what happened with the 1985 No Name Team. Our

winning ways attracted the best players from less successful teams to join our ranks, which made us even more formidable, thereby attracting still more top-notch players. And,
more recently, the very same mechanism has been at work
in helping the Navarone Team acquire its championship
level.

If you're team captain, take heed of this cycle and use it
to your advantage. And always do everything in your power
to prevent any negative, defeatist attitudes from cropping
up on your team. Even if you've been on a losing streak for
the day (or the month, for that matter), it's very important
to keep up the "fighting spirit" of your team by refusing to
allow feelings of dejection to infuse either them or you.
Momentum is crucial in paintball games, and it's much eas-
ier to both grasp and maintain momentum if your side can
keep a positive outlook.

If you can succeed in instilling a "can do" attitude in your
team, you'll be more than halfway to victory already!

★★★★★★★★★

Now let's discuss game psychology on a more individual
basis.

For starters, understand that even the most talented players will never realize their full potential when they play on
a low-caliber team. It's just too discouraging when you're
unable to count on your teammates to back you up.

If you're with a team that has the potential for success,
however, there are many ways you can increase your confidence level. And your example might inspire confident behavior in your teammates.

Experience has taught me that there are two keys to stay-
ing psyched-up and successful:

1. **Always play aggressively.**

2. **Always remember that it's just a game.**

Paintball can get real weird if taken too seriously, and some of the best players I've ever seen are also the ones who have the most good-natured, light-hearted approach to the sport. It seems obvious, but players forget the simplest fact: although paintball simulates violent gunplay, **it's not real**, and if you get shot, it's no big deal—it's part of the sport. You just say "Good shot," wipe off the mess, and get ready for the next game. Paintball is just for kicks and is very forgiving; real warfare most definitely is not.

In a later chapter, I discuss one of my favorite techniques, the "banzai charge." In real combat, it would be only on your average cold-day-in-hell when I would try such tactics. But in paintball play, the ploy gives me about an 80% success rate—very good odds for a game, but in real life, a disquieting gamble indeed . . .

The point is simple: by remembering that it's only a game, you free yourself to play very aggressively. And aggressive play is a blast! You can take the kind of risks you would never dream of in real life.

Why do rookie players demonstrate a notorious tendency to hide and do nothing? Because they're usually taking the whole damn thing too seriously! And this is one of the main reasons why it's so easy for an experienced team to trounce an inexperienced one. The beginners just hide in the bushes, anxious and frightened, while the veterans storm right over them, having a great time.

I also think this is one of the reasons that veterans of real combat often become excellent players. It's not that their past experiences prepare them for paintball. Rather, after experiencing the horrors of real war, it's easy for them to approach the whole affair in a light-hearted way. After real shooting, it's often a relief for them to participate in an enjoyable parody of their past.

If you're a neophyte player, remember to **have fun**! With the guns, camouflage clothes, and all the other militaristic trappings of the game, it can be easy for a rookie to get caught up in the fantasy. Sportsmanship and pleasure are the first casualties when the game is taken too seriously. The faster you can overcome your fears and play the game simply as an enjoyable, thrilling sport, the faster you will develop winning paintball skills.

Of course, the other side of the coin is that, although you should strive to overcome these feelings, you should always remember that they exist—and take advantage of them when your opponents display them! The simulated combat of the game often makes people play more cautiously than they should. And you should always exploit your enemy's hesitations. To paraphrase Patton: don't worry about the enemy taking advantage of your fears—let him worry about you taking advantage of his!

This is why you should always play aggressively, even on defense. An aggressive player can take advantage of a little fear to place an opponent on the defensive. Your daring alone will often cause an adversary to become unnerved and unwisely run from a favorable position.

In a later chapter, I'll discuss using loud, frightening yells as a routine part of my "banzai charges." And remember the example of the roaring attacks of the big cats? It's often best to accompany your aggressive moves with loud "war whoops" —or "Rebel Yells," as my proud Southern ancestors called them! These yells can make all the difference in your opponents' decision to either hold firm or retreat helter-skelter. And once you cause them to break ranks and retreat, you'll have a big psychological advantage over them. Whether they like it or not (or whether they admit it to themselves), they will have been *intimidated*. And that it is exactly what you want, for an intimidated adversary is, more often than not, an ineffective adversary.

Whether you are firing your gun, yelling, or charging wildly forward, a large part of the reason for your actions should be to intimidate your opponents. If you can intimidate them, they'll be halfway to defeat already!

Of course, always conduct your intimidation tactics in a spirit of fun and good sportsmanship. Aggressive play is great and can be fun for both sides. But when your opponent starts to feel that you are malicious in your intimidation and too aggressive, then the fun of the game will vanish for both of you. Healthy competition is always fun; taunting or "beating up" your opponents is rude and immature.

On an individual level, you must maintain a positive mental attitude at all times. Don't allow any temporary setbacks to upset your equilibrium or alter your basic style of play. You'll be well ahead of the game if you always take things, including your bad luck and misfortunes, in stride and refuse to let them make you distracted—and therefore vulnerable. Keeping level-headed and alert at all times is the hallmark of a good, confident player.

The individual psychology of the game is, in many ways, like gambling. Almost every move you make in a paintball game will be a calculated risk. And how accomplished a player you become will depend largely on how adept you get at making these calculations.

Other sports tend to be more forgiving—if you make a big mistake you might suffer for it, but you're still in the game. But in paintball, when you commit an error, all you can do is learn from it for the next game.

This is fundamental to the sport, and it partly explains the game's amazing growth and popularity. Paintball is, of necessity, a *thinking person's game.*

Ponder that for a moment. Experienced players will soon come to a key realization: **you are your worst enemy**. Almost every mistake you make make playing paintball is a direct result of not thinking through your tactics. Don't take dumb risks—take *calculated* risks.

In a casino, the house enjoys a set advantage on the games, but it isn't very large—5¼% on roulette, less on craps and blackjack. But these percentages alone aren't responsible for the huge profits that casinos rake in. The real advantage lies

in the fact that customers seldom quit when they logically should (that is, when they are ahead), and they keep playing until they lose their stake.

Further, the house has an enormous bankroll and can afford to ride out losing streaks, whereas players are vulnerable to being forced out of the game during extended downturns due to a lack of funds. This usually takes them out of the action at the most disadvantageous times for them, but the most favorable time for the house, since it now has all the customer's money in its pocket.

Experienced gamblers are fond of pointing out that in a casino, you're not really playing against the house—its percentage is set and immutable. You're really playing against yourself.

A gambler's biggest enemies are two different emotions, both of which originate within his own mind: greed and frustration. Greed keeps him seated at the gaming table after Lady Luck has already been generous, rather than wisely taking his winnings and quitting while he's ahead. And his frustration causes him to do even greater harm to himself when he's down. Frustration can cause him to make unwise moves, such as placing foolish bets and throwing "good money after bad," as they say. You will be in a similar position when playing paintball. There's an old soldiers' saying: Don't worry about the bullet with your name on it, because it will get you anyway. It's those marked "To Whom It May Concern" that you have to watch out for!

In paintball, you've got to accept the fact that taking risks is a large part of the game, and you will, despite your best efforts to the contrary, be eliminated often. Count on it. But to improve your game, you must focus on avoiding elimination due to bad moves and carelessness. And as you strive to improve your game, the gambler's biggest problems—greed and frustration—can easily become your two biggest enemies.

I believe that, even now, about 30% to 40% of the times that I get shot are directly attributable to my allowing one of these two emotions to overcome my better judgment. (The rest of the times occur when I make the proper moves but get shot anyway.)

Frustration has many causes: your gun isn't working right; your rookie teammates aren't moving; you've just blown an easy shot and your target escaped and you've got to chase him. Whatever the cause, learn to recognize frustration as a dangerous, destabilizing element and fight to control it. Don't let it goad you into making hasty, unwise moves. Always try to play a steady game, even when things haven't been going exactly your way.

If you feel yourself becoming frustrated, then fall back into a more cautious, reserved style of play temporarily. This will help prevent the additional frustration that comes from a careless move caused by the original frustration! Try to relax and, most importantly for your teammates, keep yourself alive and in the game. Learn to practice the "three P's" to which all good gamblers subscribe: patience, perseverance, and a positive attitude. You'll be a much better player for it.

Likewise, don't let the gambler's other nemesis, greed, affect you either.

When things have been going really well, and you've already got three or four "kills" notched on your gun handle during a game, don't get cocky! This is the time you'll have to be on your guard against treacherous feelings of overconfidence and greed. The moment you start feeling invulnerable is the moment when, suddenly, from out of nowhere—*Splat!*—you're out of there!

Don't get carried away with yourself like the foolish gambler who quickly bets away all his hard-won chips because he thinks he can do no wrong. Always try to walk away from the table while you're still ahead . . .

Since we've covered the psychological dangers you face in paintball, let's discuss some of the psychological *benefits* you can achieve from playing the sport.

For many players, the release of pent-up hostility and aggression is the main benefit of playing the game. It's really a sort of mental catharsis for many players. People who hold high-pressure, demanding jobs especially enjoy paintball, because it's a great way for them to "cut loose" and release their tensions in a harmlesss, exhilarating way.

And the pure exhilaration of the sport is another benefit. I described earlier being on a "week-long adrenaline rush" from my first game. Unfortunately, as you become a more seasoned player, this effect becomes less pronounced, but it's always present to some degree. I also advised avoiding "combat fantasies," as they can make you play more cautiously than you should. But if you enjoy getting a little caught-up in the fantasy of the situation and can use it to help you play better and more aggressively, then by all means, go for it! As long as you observe the rules and remember that it's just a game, you can fantasize away. Fantasy adds to the heart-pounding feeling of being "really alive" that many players derive from the action.

Paintball can also be a wonderful vehicle for gaining new insights into yourself. The high stress of the game often helps people to "see within themselves" in ways they never have. The games can be a metaphor for life in general, and the way you react on the field often tells how you would react to an analogous, real-life circumstance.

Another important psychological benefit from paintball is similar to the one which people derive from participating in other "thrill sports" like motorcycle racing, hang gliding, and skydiving—a release of tension.

The game gets your mind tightly wound-up for a brief time, and then you discover that you can successfully deal with the stress. It gives you a new perspective, and everyday problems that seemed so fearsome suddenly seem trivial. This naturally leads to a reduction of the tensions in your life.

The best thing about using paintball to release tension is that, unlike the other sports mentioned, the danger is mostly illusory. If you make a mistake in paintball, you get some paint on your clothes. If you make a mistake skydiving, well . . .

Still another pleasant aspect of paintball is the way it promotes laughter and humor among the players. Admittedly, some of the humor is rather dark, as the tableau of "playing war" lends itself to black (but often hilarious) comedy. During a typical day's outing, the joking and laughter seem to never cease, and this, too, adds greatly to the tension-relieving effect.

But perhaps the greatest psychological benefit of all is the one mentioned in the Introduction—the wonderful way that the game can make you feel like a kid! Cops-and-Robbers and Hide-and-Go-Seek are two types of common, exhilarating, downright fun games that children, throughout the ages, have played. And paintball combines them all!

Your mind is completely clear of all other worries as you warily stalk through the woods with all your senses alert, looking for that cunning adversary who is lurking out there somewhere and is, no doubt, hunting you with the very same fervor! With such an exciting, spine-tingling drama, your mind can't help but focus completely on the task at hand, and all your "adult" worries totally vanish, as though they never existed!

You are running, hiding, chasing, laughing like a child again, and this, in my opinion, is the best aspect of the whole experience.

Individual Roles

YOUR TEAM WILL be divided primarily into two general categories: attackers and defenders. However, there are several different roles to which players might be assigned within these two groups. In addition, some players might be designated to play *both* offense and defense during the game, depending on how it unfolds.

Defense

The defense can be divided into two categories: flag defenders and forward defenders.

The **flag defenders**, stationed in the immediate vicinity of the flag, remain pretty much stationary throughout the game, unless they must chase their stolen flag.

Forward defenders should proceed at the beginning some distance downfield and then lie in wait for approaching enemy attackers. This defense should be able to eliminate a few

adversaries—reducing the enemy's strength and confidence—before they can advance within range of the flag. Forward defenders may eventually become either attackers or flag defenders, depending on the strength and skill of the enemy offense. If pressed hard, they might need to retreat to a flag defense position. If they encounter light resistance, however, they should press forward and assist the offense in capturing the enemy flag.

Forward defenders can also be designated as a reactionary, or a "swing," squad. They can be instructed to advance just short of mid-field, wait to hear where the first firefight occurs, and then move to reinforce their buddies, preferably in a flanking maneuver.

Offense

Players on offense can also be assigned various roles. In my experience, it has proved best to create one pure assault group to maintain the greatest strength-in-numbers, but you might wish to divide it into a couple of elements. Although you can always assign one brave (or foolhardy!) individual to proceed in advance of the main force as a "scout," a good tactic is to make one-third of your assault group into the **lead troop**, with the remaining two-thirds trailing a few yards behind.

In a 12-person attack force, for example, about four players would be designated the lead troop. They should be your most seasoned veterans, since it's immensely helpful if they are friends who know each other by sight and can work as a team. Since they will serve as "brush-breakers" to locate and flush out the enemy, they should also be the most aggressive, "commando-like" players of the troop. Responsibility for maintaining the momentum of your assault will be resting on their shoulders.

In this formation, your best players are positioned up front, so they should be able to handle enemy opposition by themselves. The remainder of your group will push through from behind, flank pesky snipers, and "mop up" the area.

If, however, terrain or circumstances dictate that your attack force should remain one solid group, it can be better strategy to *reverse* the order and assign novice players to the front-line, with the hardcore veterans a few yards behind. This tactic often works well on fields with thick cover. Using this formation, you'll be unlikely to lose your best players to an ambush, and the veterans will be in an ideal location to flank opponents embroiled in firefights with the novices in front. This formation also works particularly well when there's a clear distinction between players on your team—a handful of seasoned veterans and the rest naive, but enthusiastic, greenhorns.

With this strategy, you will protect your most valuable troops, who can, in turn, keep the novices moving by yelling out encouragement and advice.

If this ploy of sending the beginners to the front-lines sounds a little cold-blooded, well hey, after all, what are rookies for?!

TACTICAL TIP #3

At the start of a game, it's a sure bet that anyone in front of you, facing your direction, is an enemy. Blast him! As the game progresses, however, you must be more cautious so you don't shoot your own teammates. Plus, you must keep a sharper eye out for enemy players sneaking up on you from behind.

Team Strategies

I N MY EXPERIENCE, the simplest strategies are always by far the best. While complicated maneuvers might look good on paper, they will invariably fail in practice for two reasons:

First, you can never get the enemy to cooperate! Never attempt a strategy that depends on the predicted actions of your opponents. They *never* do what you think they will.

Second, your team will likely be unable to execute a complicated plan properly. Even if your whole team consists of seasoned players, overly complex plays don't work because there are too many variables, too many unknowns, and too many things that can go wrong during a game. It's much better to keep the plan simple and rely on quality play.

Prior to mapping-out a strategy, the most important factor to consider is the make-up of both your team and the enemy team. Does the enemy group consist of young, athletic types capable of attacking quickly, or are they older, more sedentary players who will be more likely to play a defensive game? Or are they a mixture? How aggressive is

the opposing team's captain? Are they, or you, outnumbered?
These will be crucial points for you to ponder.

You also need to consider carefully the terrain of the field
and its layout, as these factors often dictate the wisest strategy. How thick is the vegetation? Are there any natural bot-
tlenecks on the field? Are there any water hazards or open
areas on the field?

And consider the locations of—and the avenues of approach to—the two flag stations. Are there easily negotia-
ble paths between the two, or dense cover? Are there any

strongholds that guard the approaches? How easy are they to defend? You must consider that an enemy who has an easily defendable flag station, such as one located on a sparsely covered hillside, will be able to assign more players to offense.

Carefully weigh all these complex factors, but remember, always create a simple plan based upon them.

Dividing Your Team

The most common mistake of novice paintball captains is to divide up their assault force into too many smaller units. As a general rule, unless the layout of the field dictates otherwise, I strongly recommend that you keep *all* offensive players together in one formidable attack force. There truly is strength in numbers, so take advantage of it!

Playing paintball was a matter of love at first sight for me, so after playing a few times on Mike Missile's team, I decided to create a team of my own. For our first game, I recruited 15 people. As captain, of course, I had the responsibility of planning our method of attack. (This game, as were so many others that I was to play, occurred on the lower field at L. A. Sho-Down.)

I divided our team into four "platoons," with four men assigned to each. At the time, I was reading the excellent book *The 13th Valley* by John Del Vechio, and I was enamored of a lot of military lingo, so I gave the four groups code names: *Alpha, Bravo, Delta,* and *Rover.* I told Alpha and Bravo, the two attack forces, to advance down one side of the field and hit the enemy flag from two different directions in a pincer maneuver. Delta was the defense, and Rover (which I led) was assigned a forward-defensive role. Our positions, and our proposed lines of attack, are diagrammed in the illustration on the next page.

Sixteen men, divided into four groups of four men each, for a total of eight men attacking and eight defending—all sounds very logical, doesn't it? And the twin-element pincer attack looks real impressive on paper too, huh?

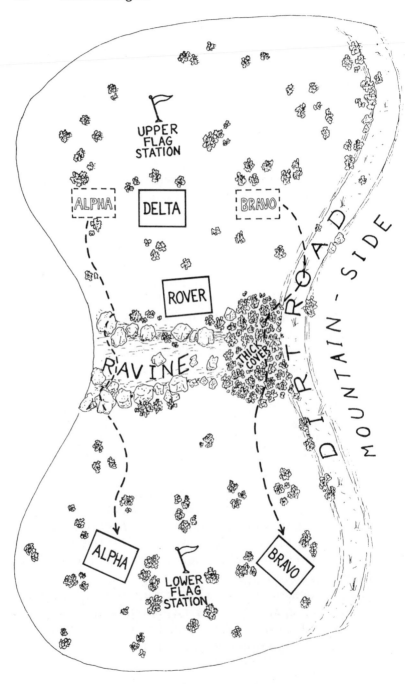

Sad to say, it wasn't too impressive during the game.

Several things are wrong with this plan. For one, the pincer idea looks good on paper, but it rarely works well in practice. Even if both units manage to get through intact, they probably won't arrive at the enemy's flag station at the same time. Plus, the two groups will have lost communication during the trip downfield. So, even if they did manage to arrive simultaneously, neither would know the other's location as they approached the enemy flag, and the groups might accidentally fire at one another (especially since players entering an enemy's flag station area tend to be paranoid and a bit trigger happy!).

It's best to advance downfield as one group and maintain uninterrupted communications the entire way.

Second mistake: I forgot the old adage that the best defense is a good offense, and I assigned too large a percentage of our force as defenders. Instead of having the Rover squad play defense, I should have incorporated them into an assault group and relied on capturing the enemy flag quickly to carry the day.

A single, 12-person attack force would have been a very formidable adversary. Unless the enemy commander had been smart enough to assemble all his attackers into a similar, large troop, such a force could have quickly overwhelmed any opposition encountered. And even if it did run up against an equally large enemy force, at least it would have had enough strength to hold its own and not be destroyed.

A large group will often annihilate smaller units, primarily because large groups can execute more effective flanking maneuvers than their outmanned opponents. And the large group has another advantage: spare players available to lay down suppressive fire while their teammates flank. Plus, thanks to the feeling of security in being a member of a big group, the larger squad will have a psychological advantage over the enemy, who is usually quite intimidated. Believe me, there's nothing as disheartening as the spectacle of a scurvy horde swarming your position!

Besides weakening our team by creating small units, I also failed to consider the terrain features. On this field, units from both teams can reach their side of the ravine at midfield at just about the same time, if they run. By ordering the Alpha team to attack along the lower side of the field, regardless of enemy opposition, I made them unnecessarily vulnerable. I should have instructed them to attack across the ravine *only* if they arrived before enemy players got to the other side. Remember, a four man squad can't afford *any* casualties.

Because of the terrain on this field—especially the bottleneck in the middle—it would have been better to consolidate the Alpha group into a large attack force, instruct two defenders from the Delta group to run to our side of the ravine, and prevent the enemy from crossing. Meanwhile, our large attack group would take care of any opponents trying to infiltrate from the high side. This concept is outlined in the next illustration.

With this strategy, we establish a solid front across the bottleneck at mid-field early in the game. We also are taking advantage of the terrain by stationing only two players on the easily defendable gulch, while allowing our attack group to remain in full force and proceed through the more problematic thick brush at the top. Notice, too, that we have placed 14, instead of the original eight, players in a position to do us immediate good.

With the full-field coverage we achieved at the bottleneck, it would have been a waste to leave more than two players back to defend the flag. Remember, the two men at the ravine can always fall back if they need to.

Considering the terrain and layout of this field, and assuming that you have a reasonably adept team, this plan is probably the best possible in these circumstances. And it

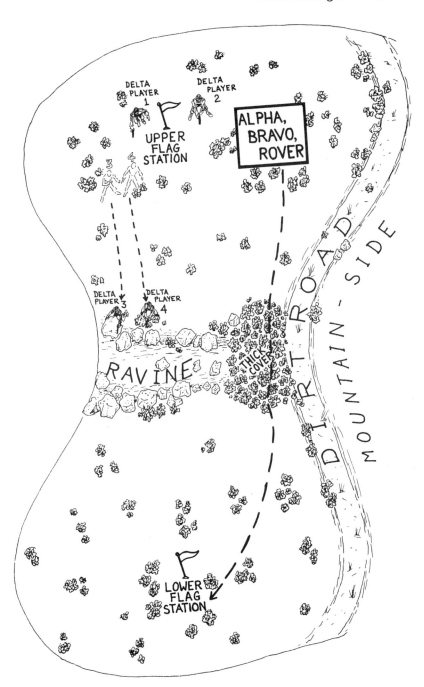

is essentially the same scheme that the championship No Name Team used most frequently on this field, under the leadership of Mike Keyes. Our only variations were that sometimes our assault group would proceed down the low side of the field just to keep the other guys guessing, and sometimes we would leave no one back to guard our flag at the outset of the game. Bill Saugez and I were often the two guys assigned as forward defenders to guard either the ravine or the high road, depending on which way our assault group went.

As the season progressed, we acquired the best players from teams we had defeated in the playoffs, and by the end of the season, we had become a real juggernaut of a team.

On a more regularly shaped field, or when matched against opponents of comparable skill, we would have been foolish to leave our flag totally unguarded. Of course, Bill and I, along with a few others, were instructed to fall back into a defensive posture if enemy players were observed intruding into our territory (a fact to which we would have been quickly alerted, thanks to the great communication on our team).

When we were playing against weak opponents, often everyone would join the assault group and go after the flag. We implemented all the techniques stressed in this book—constant communication, firing, flanking, proper teamwork—and we attained astounding victories. On several occasions, we totally annihilated the enemy team without suffering a single casualty ourselves!

Sometimes in such games, for good practice, we would treat a firefight that occurred around the enemy flag station like any other combat that might occur at mid-field. We ignored the flag and concentrated on eliminating all our opponents in the area. Then, when the opposition was thoroughly mopped up, Donald Keyes (who sometimes wore a clown suit along with a huge, fluorescent wig just to mess with our adversaries' minds!) would waltz in and pose for a picture by the flag before he pulled it!

Such arrogance, huh? But it was the kind of stuff that builds a genuine, good-hearted *esprit de corps.*

Summary

Of course, if you play on a field in Kansas, or Florida, or New York, you might be wondering how my explaining the best tactics for one field in Southern California can benefit you. Well, I've analyzed the best maneuvers on this one field simply to illustrate some general concepts.

First, I demonstrated how terrain features often dictate the most advantageous strategy to undertake.

Second, I showed you the importance of strength-in-numbers. The violation of this maxim is the main mistake beginners make time and time again. And it's the error that I'd most like you to avoid.

In general, the best advice I can give is to carefully consider all the questions mentioned at the beginning of this chapter as they apply to your field. Then, taking into account the strength-in-numbers concept and considering the wisest use of your available players, formulate a *simple* plan of attack. It can be as simple as "two guys back, everyone else straight up the middle to attack their flag station as quickly as possible." As long as everyone understands what the plan is and how it's appropriate to the field, your team should do very well.

In the above examples, "our" team has been better than or equal to its opponent. But what should you do if you're badly outnumbered or outclassed—or, worse yet, both?

First, don't despair. There are ways to overcome both these handicaps, especially if you're simply outnumbered. Being outclassed is, admittedly, more of a problem, but you can mitigate this disadvantage also.

If You're Outclassed

If the other team has more skilled players than yours, the strength-in-numbers idea becomes crucial. Splitting your troops into small units will just turn them into shark bait for their seasoned foes. It's much better to keep them in one group. Though they still might get chewed, at least the enemy will have to work for it and suffer a few casualties in the process. And it will probably buy you some time as well.

If you've been badly beaten once or twice, or if you're simply playing a team with a fearsome reputation, consider this: they might be over-confident. Especially if you've just played a few games and none of your force has been able to penetrate their territory, you should suspect that they'll leave only one or two players back to defend their flag. After all, who on their team would volunteer to hang back and be bored silly defending a flag that no one will attack?

In this case, try the following strategy:

Assign all of your men to defense except two to four of your best, most physically fit players. Station your defenders to provide the strongest possible protection for your flag. Also, send a few to mid-field at the start with orders to harass the approaching enemy, but fall back quickly if necessary. Instruct your small assault group (we refer to such players as "snakes") to run as far downfield as they safely can but stop just short of mid-field, where they should hide, listen, and try to locate the enemy attack force (who will probably be noisy at this point). Then they should either hide until the enemy passes or, if feasible, sneak around them.

The snakes must *avoid* enemy contact and go to all lengths to conceal themselves. If they blunder into the enemy at mid-field, they should retreat to conceal their true intent, and then sneak around to the sides. Their main job, until they see the enemy flag, is to *survive*. If they can make it to the flag undetected, they might be able to waltz right in and grab a totally unguarded flag!

If there are defenders at the flag, however, the snakes

should strike quickly and aggressively. One tactic is to suppress the defenders, if they can't be easily eliminated, while the fastest man dashes in to pull the flag.

If there are enemy defenders alive after the flag is stolen, one snake should either stay back to keep them occupied or else sprint out of the area after the flag carrier has departed, and then lag a few steps behind and keep a sharp watch to the rear after he has rejoined the assault group.

The snakes should proceed back downfield as quickly as possible, continuing to avoid enemy contact. They should also have a special password to announce their return to teammates at their home flag station, and they should approach very cautiously if, upon their successful return, they hear a firefight nearby.

This strategy might work only once, but it'll sure make the other guys treat you with more respect. Even one victory can be a great morale-booster to a team that's beginning to despair!

If You're Outnumbered

If you're simply outnumbered, try the "delayed assault" tactic. (It also may work if you're outclassed.) I'll explain it in terms of the way we successfully employed it at Bushwhackers—one of my favorite fields—located in the northwestern end of the San Fernando Valley in a town called Moorpark, California. The field is diagrammed in the illustration on the next page.

The cover, generally thick with a lot of saplings and bamboo, has quite a few open areas as well, notably the shallow but wide river located at mid-field. In fact, it's the river that makes this field so interesting and so much fun to play. Everyone loves splashing across it!

Anyway, on this day, Peter was the team captain. We were outnumbered 24 to 17, though we had the better players. We had lost the first two games, and we needed to win three straight to win for the day. The third game, thanks to Peter's smart planning, became our "turn-around" game. Here's

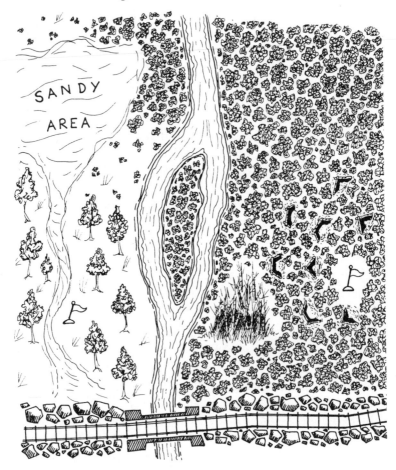

how we played it:

We knew we were outnumbered, but in this game we had the more easily defensible side of the field, so we decided to hold our entire force on our side of the river for at least the first half of the game (it's important to keep close track of the time with these types of tactics) and then take advantage of our strong position to shoot up the enemy assault group(s). Since the enemy had the side of the field that was harder to defend, we figured the opposing team's captain would leave at least seven defenders back, possibly more.

We hoped we would, at worst, face an equal number of attackers on our side of the field—and we would have the stronger positions.

The plan worked perfectly.

Our opponents threw two eight-man assault groups at us, and we shot both of them up pretty badly. Peter and I shot over half of one group ourselves, as we played "Cong tactics" and hid in a clump of bamboo. They knew where we were, but they couldn't dislodge us, and they lost three players plus 15 or 20 minutes in their attempt.

The remaining attackers, in exasperation, decided to advance against our flag, leaving one guy back to keep an eye on us. Peter caught this joker napping, however, and then we had ourselves a field day! We came in behind the intruders, who were engaged in a firefight with our flag defenders—they were unaware of our presence until it was too late, and we picked them off one by one.

Our original plan had been to send an assault party across the river after 30 minutes had elapsed. But after discussion, we determined that we were so far ahead on body-count that we stayed on our side of the river and waited for the eight enemy flag defenders to get bored and come over after us. After all, we had suffered very few casualties, and since we had them outnumbered about 2-to-1 at this point, we knew they'd be easy pickings when they came. And they were!

Our victory in this game boosted team morale considerably, and we went on to win the next two games and came away with a victory for the day.

One play I should caution you about is the all-out, hell-bent-for-leather, balls-to-the-wall, kamikaze-style attack. Kamikazes occasionally work. If you're playing on a short field where this type of attack is more likely and you suspect your enemy is planning an all-out attack, you might want to hold your assault group back at your flag station at the start of a game, because kamikazes often succeed against a lightly defended flag.

However, kamikazes usually fail, because momentum is everything in these attacks, and momentum is easily lost. For a kamikaze attack to succeed, there must be *total* commitment from every member of the attack force, and often this is lacking. It's senseless—and discouraging—for the forward players to sacrifice themselves charging an enemy position and then witness their teammates, who were supposed to be rushing in right behind them, scampering into the brush for cover.

Another great danger to momentum is paint checks—they can ruin the entire charge. Every player should be warned in advance that he must renew the kamikaze assault immediately after the referee resumes play.

If you're contemplating a kamikaze attack, make it crystal clear to all players that it's a total go-for-broke situation and that the game will be won or lost within a matter of minutes.

Played correctly, kamikaze attacks can make for some real fun games because of the fast, furious shoot-outs and because, win or lose, the entire team can return to the field within minutes, ready for the next game!

★★★★★★★★★

A final bit of advice on team strategy: a team should always strive to play its own game and not its opponent's. If your team has been succeeding with one style of play or a certain type of strategy then, by all means, stick to it!

If your team has been experiencing success by playing aggressively, for example, stay with aggressive tactics and take advantage of your natural strength in this area. If, on the other hand, your team lacks the necessary quickness and stamina to do well offensively, but it has a history of strong defense, then stick with defensive strategies.

The point is, never play into your opponents' hands by changing the aspect of your game that has paid-off for you in the past, just because you perceive a strength on their side. Further, don't radically alter your basic, tried-and-true game plans because you think you're suddenly playing a "better" team than you've faced in the past.

If you've been winning all season with decisive attacks and aggressive play, don't abandon this concept and try to play defensively just because you're facing a higher caliber opponent.

Of course, you should adjust your style of play *somewhat* in response to different fields or different opponents, but always basically stick with whatever game works best for your team. To do otherwise would be arguing with success. And that could be the best thing you could do—for your enemy!

TACTICAL TIP #4

It's very beneficial for you and your team to play on as many different fields as possible, especially if you're involved in serious competition. Playing in different environments will give you adaptability and make you a much better all-around player.

Playing as a Team

REGARDLESS OF THE plan of attack you use, the most critical factor for success will be your players' **teamwork**.

All the techniques previously discussed—moving, communicating, flanking, etc.—depend on proper coordination and cooperation between team members. The best individual player on earth will accomplish little without good support from his teammates. And without proper teamwork, a large troop will lose its strength-in-numbers advantage—and become nothing but a large target for the enemy.

A first-class paintball team will be, like a work of fine art, greater than the sum of its parts.

When I played with the No Name Team in 1985, we had some outstanding individual players, but they did not carry us to the Nationals. The reason we had such a great season was that we played *as a team*.

When one of us charged forward to a new position, we

knew that our teammates would be backing us up from behind. When one of us was embroiled in a shoot-out with an
opponent, we knew—without having to ask—that our buddies were already stalking and flanking to eliminate him.
When one of us dashed from the enemy base camp with a
stolen flag, we knew that our partners would cover our
retreat. If one of us had to sacrifice ourselves to accomplish
an important goal, we left the field knowing that our com-
panions would take proper advantage of our elimination.

All this gave us a level of confidence unmatched by our
competitors. And confidence, as you will remember from
the chapter on psychology, is the key to success in this sport.

The most practical advice I can give is simple common
sense: *assign your players into units where members know
each other well.*

Of course, this won't always be possible. But you must try,
because people who are familiar with each other will function as teammates much more smoothly than strangers. Obviously, communication—the cornerstone of teamwork—is
greatly enhanced when players can call to each other by
name. After all, "Hey you!" is an embarrassing, and often
ineffective, salutation between people who are supposed to

be teammates!

It goes a lot deeper than that, however. Cooperation and teamwork are basic human needs. Teamwork allowed our primitive ancestors to evolve quickly and successfully into the masters of their environment.

Our distant relatives were—as we still are today—rather frail creatures compared to the big carnivores with whom they shared the plains and the jungles. By working together, however, early hunters were able to overcome their more formidable adversaries. They managed to survive and thrive by banding together into tribes. The kinship and bonding between members did not apply to outsiders, who were probably often considered "enemies."

In the modern world, your "tribe" consists of your relatives and close friends, wherever they may be located. These are the people with whom you feel most comfortable. You are familiar with their personalities and know what to expect from them. They are also the people whom you care the most for and would go to the greatest lengths to defend.

When members of a paintball team are friends, magic will happen: individual players will learn to function as one unit, rather than as disjointed parts. And this is the stuff of which superior teams are made!

Another thing that builds team spirit is to have everyone equipped with the same type of uniform and/or insignia. It will build unity as well as aid in on-field recognition among your players.

It is also very important that dissension be kept to a minimum. Since paintball games are sporting contests, there will always be some second-guessing, but it should be discouraged. There's nothing worse than getting the 30-second warning from the judge before the game starts, and then having players question the plan of attack, with a dozen guys competing to see who can voice his brilliant plan the loudest!

As I said before, it doesn't matter so much *what* your plan is, as long as it is relatively simple and understood by everyone. Team captains need not be dictators, but they must insure that everyone agrees on one play so the team can work together.

If the start of the game is at hand and your team members have been unable to reach a consensus, the captain *must* take command and decide on a strategy. Though you might hesitate to do this because you're afraid you'll feel like the goat if you lose, you must make *some* decision, or you'll lose anyway. Your victories—which I hope will be plentiful—will more than make up for your losses, believe me.

TACTICAL TIP #5

Purchase your own paintball gun. Having your own weapon with which you're thoroughly familiar will increase your accuracy dramatically. Playing with rental guns is like playing baseball with someone else's glove—it might be functional, but it just won't have the right "feel" to it.

Defending the Flag

AS I'M SURE you know by now, I believe the best defense is a good offense. Plus, aggressive play makes games more fun and action-packed. Nothing is more boring than two defense-oriented teams wasting away an hour of game time, with the only action being a little long-distance sniping between forward units.

I remember one game in the 1985 NSG North American Championships between two defensive teams. The game was a battle between the defending champions from the previous year—the Atlanta Blue Team and the Over-The-Hill Gang from Mississippi (which went on to win the tournament and the championship that year). The highlight of the story, however, is that this game went 58 minutes without a single casualty!

Finally, with only about 90 seconds remaining, someone from the Mississippi team scored a hit against an Atlanta player, thereby eking out a narrow victory for his side. If he hadn't made that shot, both teams would have been

declared losers for that game of the double-elimination tournament. Needless to say, good flag defense didn't make a bit of difference to the outcome of that game!

However, in a well-balanced game between two aggressive teams, proper flag defense is an important—sometimes crucial—element of play.

Stationing Flag Defenders

I've never enjoyed playing strict flag defense, because it can be tedious to hide in one spot and wait for the enemy to show up. I have, however, had some very fun games playing forward defense, where you're free to give ground. And, since you're playing against enemy assault groups, your opponents are obliged to come to you! I love to retreat after an enemy encounter and set up another ambush, and I really enjoy the "ninja" tactics you can employ in a forward defense position.

However, there will likely be a few members on your team who want to play strict flag defense. You can always ask for volunteers at the start of the game. (You'll probably get more and more volunteers as the day wears on and the physical exertions take their toll!)

If available manpower permits, station at least two play-ers with a clear shot at your flag pole. Leaving just one per-son can be too risky, since the outcome of the whole game could come down to just one shot at a rushing enemy as-saulter. And leaving just one player with a clear shot at the flag also leaves it vulnerable to a two-man rush, especially if it's located in a small clearing with thick cover nearby (into which a second man could duck before you had time to reload). To further protect themselves and the flag against this possibility, the two defenders should agree ahead of time who will fire first and who will fire second, in case two or more enemies rush the flag simultaneously.

Other available defenders should be stationed in the strongest positions possible along the enemy's most likely routes of approach. (Also, if there's a lot of field behind your flag station, don't forget to be alert for the enemy coming in from behind!) When I refer to "strong positions," I mean behind or in the thickest cover available that still allows a broad field of fire.

Having the largest possible field of fire is especially im-portant to you as a defensive player, because the enemy, not you, will dictate the terms of the confrontation. As the as-saulters invade your area, they will make the moves, and you will be reacting to them. Since you can never predict exact-ly where they'll invade, station yourself where you can train your weapon on as much of the field as possible.

If you have the time, put yourself in your enemy's boots by walking out from your flag station and viewing the ap-proaches from an assaulter's perspective. Looking at things from their viewpoint might give you insight into placing your defense in the most difficult positions for your opponents.

The illustration depicts the near-flag station at the field *Survival South* in Rhode Island. The five players in the dia-gram occupy the positions that I would choose if I were in charge of flag defense there. It also shows their fields of fire:

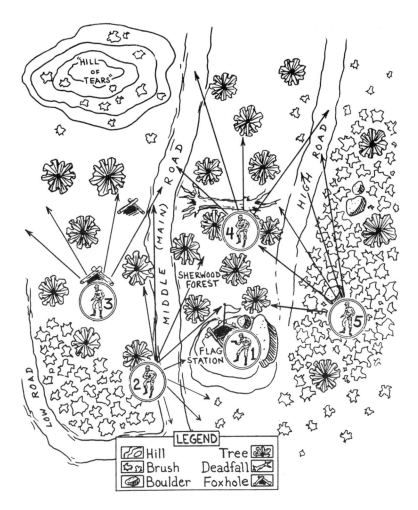

- *Player #1*, in a strong defensive position behind solid cover (boulders), is right on top of the flag and is also somewhat elevated, giving himself a good look-out post.

- *Player #2* also has a good shot at the flag pole (although from a little more distance), a clear view, and an open shot down the middle road. Plus, he can guard against players sneaking around to the rear of the flag station via the low road.

- *Player #3* has a strong position in the bunker, a good view of the main road, and at least a long shot at the flag pole. In this position, he commands a wide field of fire and presents a major obstacle to an enemy assault group trying to advance down the left flank.

- *Player #4*, also commanding a large field of fire, is behind solid cover and can view both the main and the high roads.

- *Player #5*, although he doesn't have a clear field of fire through the thick brush, is behind solid cover and can help stall an enemy advance through the thick stuff on the right flank. He is also in a rather good ambush position, especially against players advancing down the high road.

Of course, each field is unique, and I've furnished this only as a general example. However, study the use of terrain and the interlocking fields of fire, and apply them to your particular field.

A good defensive position, if it doesn't severely restrict your field of fire, is inside a large bush thick enough to shield you from incoming pellets. If you can still see out and reach out to fire your gun, it could be a very strong position, since the enemy will have a tough time digging you out. Often, players in this position can be eliminated only by a "banzai" charge into the bush itself or by a player crawling to the bottom edge of the bush to shoot at the defender's ankles.

Getting the Flag Back

One thing that flag defenders **must** do is give chase if the enemy acquires your flag. Your job is **not** over when the flag is stolen! If the enemy flag carrier successfully exits the area of your flag, you can bet that he's hauling ass back to his home base. And you've got to haul your ass after him!

If they're smart, your opponents will leave a few players behind at your flag station after the rest have departed with your flag. They will try to prevent the possible successful return of your assault group. If this is the case, all the surviving flag defenders might not be able to dash after their stolen flag, but as many as possible certainly should! And if all of the enemy assaulters *do* depart with the flag carrier, then all of the flag defenders should go after them! After all, there's not much sense in guarding a portion of the field that your opponents are no longer interested in.

Finally, a team should always have a code word or phrase that defenders can shout to signify that the flag has been stolen. If they are alerted in time, your offense can try to intercept the enemy flag carrier as he's making the trip back downfield. Of course, if no code words—such as "Momma's gone!"—have been designated, simply yell "They've got the flag!" or "They've got the blue team's flag!" as loud as you possibly can. Then go get it back!

TACTICAL TIP #6

In paintball, it's not against the rules to lie! Of course, don't lie about whether you've been marked with paint, but it's OK to respond to the question, "Hey, are you on the Blue Team?" with a resounding, "Yes!" even though you're on the Red Team. And if your opponent believes you, it's perfectly within the rules to plug him and then laugh about it! Conversely, watch out for these tricks yourself and don't fall for them. Having team passwords is often helpful, but "Oingo" answered with "Boingo" is not a good one . . .

Stealing the Flag

A SUCCESSFUL FLAG capture usually results from a good mixture of wariness and a degree of recklessness. Flag assaulters *must* be aggressive, or they will never reach the enemy flag pole. Seasoned players, however, will temper their "damn the torpedoes" attitude by applying the proper amount of caution as well.

Since assault groups need to steal the flag as quickly as possible, you can employ a couple of rules-of-thumb as you advance toward the enemy flag.

First, there's the obvious fact that the first half of the field is yours for the taking at the start of the game. In other words, since both teams start at opposite ends of the field, you know that if you run like hell you can make it at least to mid-field before you need to worry about enemy players.

Second, after you cross mid-field, the likelihood of encountering enemy defenders increases proportionately to your proximity to the flag. Therefore, your level of caution and

alertness should gradually increase as you get closer to the enemy flag, and the speed of your advance should probably decrease just a little. (But never slow enough that you lose your momentum, which is of paramount importance in an offensive maneuver.)

If you make it to within rushing distance of the flag without having encountered enemy players, you should be extremely wary, as flag defenders almost certainly will be lurking in the area. Of course, it's always possible that a team has left its flag unguarded, but don't bet your life on it!

Flag-Grabbing Techniques

The proper approach that an assault group should take to nab the enemy flag will depend on how many defenders are in the area, how many assaulters you have, and what the defensive situation is around your flag pole. Plus, you should consider what, if anything, has happened during your trip downfield.

In many ways, it will be like a football game. If you're well ahead in points, you can afford to play more conservatively, but if you're losing, you'll have to take more chances and go for the "big play." Let's describe a few examples:

If your group travels easily downfield without meeting much resistance and then comes up against a heavily defended flag, you'll know that the enemy has opted for a defensive game plan. Therefore, you can afford to proceed more slowly and cautiously toward the flag, because there's probably not much offense against your flag. (This, of course, assumes that you've left your flag station reasonably defended. If you've left it only lightly guarded, you'll have to attack fast anyway.)

On the other hand, suppose you advanced downfield with a large assault group and encountered few, if any, enemy players along the way. You then discovered a lightly defended enemy flag, which you took quickly and easily. What does this tell you?

Well, you should figure that a large enemy assault group has attacked your flag and probably acquired it. In this case, you'll have to play a little differently. You'll probably want to assign a handful of your best (and fastest) players to run the enemy's flag to your base as quickly as possible. Then, station the rest of your men where they can defend the enemy flag station against adversaries returning with your flag.

Meeting Resistance

What happens when you lead an assault group downfield that *does* encounter a lot of resistance? Your tactics will depend largely on the results of the confrontations.

If you run into a large contingent of opponents somewhere near mid-field at the start of the game, you can assume that they are the enemy assault force. If all goes well and you inflict heavy casualties on them while suffering few on your side, then you'll be in a comfortable position. You will have crippled their offensive threat while racking up a substantial lead in body-count.

In this case, you'll be able to proceed a little more thoughtfully. You might even decide to abandon your plans to steal the flag and fall back into a defensive posture, since you know that your adversaries must play total offense if they hope to win. A lot will depend on how important that particular game is to you (such as whether it's part of a sanctioned competition), and on how much you just want to have fun. If you're playing strictly for the heck of it then, by all means, go after their flag! You'll probably have more fun.

What if your assault group encounters a large enemy force and they nearly wipe you out, so that only you and a few buddies are left? Well, this is where you'll be "third and long, with only one minute to play."

In this instance, you *must* play recklessly and aggressively, since you'll need the "big play" (i.e., a flag capture and return) to secure a victory. Plus, think of what a hero you'll be if you pull it off! You won't have much to lose, and it's better to go out with a roar than a whimper!

The Time Factor

You'll also need to consider how much time is left in the game and how many points a flag capture is worth on that particular field. If the capture is worth many more points than individual players, and you're way behind on body-count with the time about to expire, consider making a desperate "kamikaze" charge with *all* your surviving teammates, in a last-ditch attempt to secure at least a capture and gain some points.

Try to develop a code word that signals such an attack, but if you haven't, and if your team is too spread out to whisper instructions, you'll just have to shout out orders. Of course, this will alert the enemy flag defenders, but if they are rookies it might unnerve them a little, too. On the other hand, if they're experienced, shouting will just warn them of your impending assault, and you'll just have to live (or, more likely, die) with it.

Attacking the Flag Station

One play I like is to send one player screaming into the enemy flag station a split second before the rest of the group charges. This makes the enemy defenders fire their weapons at him, and the rest of you can use the two or three seconds it will take them to reload to eliminate some of them and grab the flag.

In fact, I believe that most flag pull attempts should be accompanied by terrifying screams! Unless you know for a fact that all defenders have been eliminated from the area (and this will seldom be the case), you should always rush the flag assuming that at least one enemy will fire a desperate, hit-or-miss shot at you. So, I urge you to charge-in screaming like a maniac to unnerve your opponents and disrupt their aim. Believe me, a target running at top speed and screaming his head off is very difficult to hit—no matter how close!

You should hit the open area around the flag at a flat-out run, and you should be in and out so fast that any enemy defenders will get only one shot apiece at you before you've vanished back into the brush. Sometimes, if I have good support in the area, I will lay down my gun before rushing the flag to give myself a little extra speed. I rely on my vocal cords to blow the defense away!

If more than two enemy defenders have a close shot at the flag pole, I don't recommend individual attempts to steal the flag, since the odds will be too heavily stacked against you. If there's just one defender left, however, and if he's under fire or some other type of pressure from your teammates, he will be vulnerable to a single-man rush from a quick player who can often get in, snatch the flag, and disappear before the defender knows what's going on.

The Two-Man Rush

If there are still two or three defenders left with a shot at the flag and you need to acquire it quickly, a tactic to try is the one I warned you about in the previous chapter—the "two-man rush."

Two players who are within easy sprinting distance of the flag can make a coordinated charge. The first player agrees to sacrifice himself and fire a couple shots so that his team-mate can acquire the flag. The first man will take off scream-ing right at the flag pole, but he must **not** touch the flag himself. He can stop in front of the flag to block shots with his body, charge an enemy position, or just rush right on through the area. But he must come close enough to the flag to make the enemy think that he's trying to steal it—and thereby make them empty their guns at him.

The second assaulter will come charging through an instant behind his buddy. If his timing is right, he can dash through the most vulnerable area around the flag pole during the second or two that it will take the enemy to reload. This two-man rush technique is depicted in the illustrations.

Leaving Players Behind

Regardless of how your group manages to acquire the flag, you must decide whether to leave players in the area of the enemy flag to guard against returning enemy flag carriers. Your decision should be based on the number of flag defenders you have encountered, the size of the enemy's offensive force, and your guess on their odds of quick success. Whatever you decide, make your decisions quickly, as time will be crucial.

If you've completely secured the enemy flag station, you should almost always leave at least one player back to ambush their flag pole, just in case an enemy flag carrier returns with your flag.

But if your group has managed to snatch the flag while there are still several enemy defenders in the area, then your *entire group* might want to depart at once to provide maximum protection for your flag carrier and to insure that he can make the journey as quickly as possible. In this case, it's very important to have a few players lag back slightly to defend against opponents who might rush in from behind. And don't forget to keep at least one player beside your flag carrier at all times to grab the flag immediately from him in case he gets shot!

Coming Home

As your group enters your home flag area, use a code word

to announce your successful return. And you should also be alert to the possibility that the enemy has ambushed *your* flag station!

It's possible that you will return to your flag station during a firefight between your defenders and an enemy assault group. In this case, determine (either visually or verbally) whether your flag is missing. If it's gone, charge right in and hang the enemy flag on your pole *immediately*, lest your opponents beat you to the punch on the opposite end of the field! You should probably have all your players cluster around your flag carrier to provide a "human shield" as he rushes in to hang the flag.

Of course, if there's a firefight in progress but your flag remains on its pole, you might decide to play more conservatively. Or, you can even **let** the enemy steal your flag so they'll vacate the area, allowing you to run in and hang their flag after they depart!

TACTICAL TIP #7

Use your ears as well as your eyes. Be attuned to your sense of hearing at all times, for it can warn you of unseen danger. If you're in a secure spot, try closing your eyes for a few minutes and concentrating only on your sound perception.

Don't Say "I'm Hit!" (Prematurely): *Elaboration on Paint Checks*

I N ADDITION TO the "Big Three" discussed previously, there is a fourth big error that rookies habitually commit: taking themselves out the game when they haven't actually been marked.

All too often, a small amount of paint will splatter on a rookie's goggles, or perhaps a pellet will bounce off his back, and in his nervousness he will yell out, "I'm hit!"—and then it's all over for that game. Of course, the rookie has not *really* been hit, and a closer examination reveals this. But by then, it's too late.

Remember how in the "Rules of the Game" chapter I briefly explained the purpose of **paint checks**? Well, the paint check rules are probably the most important rules in the whole game, and I will now discuss them more fully.

Some fields handle paint checks differently than others, so always pay close attention to the pre-game orientation lectures to familiarize yourself with any variations that apply to that particular field. I will, however, explain the paint

check rules that most commonly occur. Any differences you might encounter probably will be trivial.

Basically, a paint check is paintball's version of "time out." It's called to determine whether a player has indeed been marked with a sufficient amount of paint to qualify for elimination. A paint check may be called by the player in question, by any other player—friend or foe—in the area, or by a judge.

Once a paint check has been called, all players in the immediate vicinity (usually defined as the area within easy hearing distance) must observe it. Players affected by the paint check must immediately *cease firing* and hold their positions.

You are, however, permitted to do several things while under a paint check. You may reload pellets, change your CO_2, clean your gun, or communicate with other players. Indeed, if you suspect that the paint check will last for a few moments, it will be an opportune time to do these things. But, you cannot move from your position or fire your weapon!

If a judge is in the area—such as when a paint check is called around a flag station—he usually will conduct the examination himself. His decisions are, of course, final. When a paint check is called in an area where a judge is not nearby, then the players themselves do the check.

If you're unsure about a hit, you can often make a quick inquiry without resorting to stopping the action with a paint check. If two players are firing at one another from behind cover, and one player thinks he hit the other player, he might simply yell out, "Hey, did that get you?" If the other player has felt a pellet hit him on an area of his body that he can clearly see, but he has taken a careful look and found no paint, he might yell back, "Nope, it hit me but bounced off."

The other player probably would take his word for it and continue the game without interruption. He would, however, have the *right* to call a paint check if he felt he had good reason. But, paintball players are, for the most part, very honest, and a paint check probably would be unnecessary.

If there were some paint on the player, or if the pellet had hit him in a hard-to-see area, he probably would call a paint check on himself. If a teammate were nearby, he could check it. If no teammates were close, he might ask the enemy player to check it. In that case, both players would leave their positions and walk into the open for one to check the other.

If you have been struck solidly with a pellet that has burst, you usually will have an "splat" of paint on you equal to the size of a fifty-cent coin, and there will be no question as to whether you're hit. Other times, you may have been only lightly sprayed with paint, so you will still be in the game.

However, there is a gray area called *splatters*, where a substantial quantity of paint might have landed on you after the pellet first burst on some inanimate object, like a twig or branch. Generally, if the amount of paint is doubtful, the splattered player should be declared still alive. After all, no one likes leaving a game unless he has been eliminated fair and square.

In the rare event that players can't reach an agreement, both players may put on their elimination vests and proceed to the nearest judge for arbitration. This is the only instance, besides injury, where players may put on their elimination vests without declaring themselves out of the game.

Regardless of the verdict of the inspection, all players who are still alive are required—and *entitled*—to return to the position they held when the paint check was first called. The game can resume only after all players have had sufficient time to assume their previous positions and yelled "O.K." Then a judge or a player should yell, "Resume!"

By the way, you can't inspect a player who has relinquished his cover for a paint check, find none, and then suddenly yell "Resume!" and shoot him from two feet away! That's hardly sporting!

Paint checks evolved in paintball to assure that a player who has been eliminated fairly does not have the chance to continue playing, thereby eliminating opposing players and unfairly influencing the game.

After all, if you discovered post-game that a player had, in fact, been eliminated during the very first firefight of the game, there would be no equitable way to redress the imbalance. Paint checks help the games flow smoothly and keep everyone honest. If there's a question about a hit, members from the opposing team can always call a paint check and walk over and take a look for themselves!

Remember, "paint check" and "resume" are **magic words**. They stop and start all action in the immediate area. If you think you might have been hit and you yell, "Paint check!" and then you are hit moments later by a pellet fired by a player who either didn't hear or didn't observe your paint check, then the second pellet does **not** count.

(Note: These rules relate to everyday, "fun" games. In many tournament-level games, a paint check is *only* a request for a judge to come to the area, and it does *not* stop the action or make the player safe from further fire. Always study carefully the rules of the tournament before you play.)

There are two other magic phrases that pertain directly to paint checks: *"I'm hit!"* and *"I'm out!"* However, don't yell these phrases too hastily, because once you say, "I'm hit" or "I'm out" (or any other phrase that indicates you're out of the game), then you **are**. You can't yell, "Hit!" and then, upon seeing that the pellet didn't burst, yell, "Naw, it didn't break, I'm still in the game!" *There is no going back.*

Once you say you're out, you're out!

Why is this rule so strict? Simple. When you say you've been eliminated, you take away the aggressiveness of the player attacking you. He's probably a nice guy, and he stopped shooting at you once you said you were hit. (In fact, the rules *required* him to stop shooting at you.) So it would be grossly unfair for you to take advantage of his good sportsmanship by reneging on your earlier statement, especially after you've had time to take cover.

Depending on the brand of pellets and the weather conditions (you tend to have more "bouncers" during cold, dry weather than when it is hot and humid), nearly half the pellets that land "on target" can fail to burst. Yet, time and time again, I would eliminate rookies who, after feeling my pellet strike them, would too quickly blurt out those magic words— "I'm hit!"

If you're a novice player, train yourself not to yell out, "Hit!" until you've had time to verify the fact. Also, never stand in the open to inspect yourself, since any wise opponent will be hurling more rounds your way until you say, "Hit!"

So, if you feel a pellet strike you and you can't tell whether it broke, first dive for cover and then yell, "Paint check!" to stop the action.

I have conditioned myself to simply say "Ow!" when a pellet hits me. This usually makes my opponent pause, but it's a completely noncommittal expression.

One other important point to remember—never take yourself out of a game based on a hasty report from the enemy. If you are in a close shoot-out situation, don't take his word for it that you have been marked, even if you've felt the pellet strike you. If he yells, "Gotcha!" then you may yell, "Paint check!" to stop the action, but you shouldn't automatically respond with, "O. K., I'm hit."

Here's another benefit of the paint check rule, and one that you should take advantage of: Paint checks give you a "safe time" to ascertain the truth. If you are in an intense, point-blank shoot-out, you're not going to have time to check the validity of any hits until someone calls "Paint check" or admits his elimination. If your opponent yells, "Gotcha!" or "You're hit!" in such circumstances, you have the option of calling a paint check or continuing to fire, since such phrases have no real significance, according to the rules of the game. If you felt a pellet strike you, or if you saw a pellet burst on your opponent, then you should call a paint check. If not, you would be wise to continue firing.

Remember, the **only** words or phrases that have any real consequence in a paintball are *hit, out* (or *dead*), *paint check*, and *resume*. The proper, judicious use of these words are the hallmarks of an accomplished player.

A final thought: I know it sounds repetitive, but it can't be stressed enough—paintball is *only a game*. Play honestly, and play for fun. Don't be a sleaze and abuse the paint check rule when you know damn well you've been hit. And *always* give your opponent the benefit of the doubt. If he says the pellet didn't break, believe him and keep playing.

Don't let this great game deteriorate into a childish cursing match between you and your foe. Just use the tactics described in this book, maneuver around him, and nail him squarely with your next shot!

Do's and Don'ts of the Banzai Charge

"Damn the welts! Full speed ahead!" — Bill Barnes

BACK IN THE "old days" when I first started playing paintball, we played with Nel-Spots equipped with a bolt-action on the left side of the chamber. They were rather awkward to operate, and sometimes it would take an inexperienced player a full four seconds (or longer) to reload his weapon. (This was before anyone in our area had developed a pump mechanism to work the bolt, which made reloading much faster.)

Since I'd had some martial arts training, I realized that I could eliminate many opponents if I waited for them to fire and then immediately charge them while screaming (or *ki-ing*, as it's known in the martial arts) to startle them and make it more difficult for them to reload. I would then run up and shoot them in the chest from point-blank range!

Often, in their haste, the enemy would fail to get a pellet in his chamber and just shoot air at me, or else burst a pellet in his gun while trying to reload and just shoot harmless spray. And even if he did manage to reload a pellet, he would often miss, even at point-blank range, because my screaming would freak him out so much. I guess some of them thought that I'd just had a "flashback" or something and was about to physically attack them!

I called this tactic **the banzai charge**.

With time and practice, I became quite adept at the technique and actually got most of my kills during the early part of my paintball career this way. I improved my timing to the point where I instinctively knew how close I had to get to be within "range," and I learned how to draw fire, to catch my foe with an empty gun, without needlessly exposing myself. I eventually got so good that, unless he had a companion right by his side, anyone who fired at me from close range was a certain goner!

Of course, when pumps were added to Nel-Spots throughout southern California, the glory days of the banzai charge ended. After I'd been plugged square in the chest a few times while charging people, I had to learn to adjust to the much briefer "window of vulnerability" available for a banzai charge. Actually, it made me a better player overall, since I had relied on the banzai too much and was forced to develop some other skills.

Although the addition of pumps to most paintball guns may have quickened the average reloading time and thereby decreased the number of times you can use this tactic, the banzai charge is still a useful attack and definitely should be learned.

Two Key Points

There are two things to remember when making a banzai charge:

First, the scream is *imperative*. Especially since pumps

are so prevalent, you need to make your opponent as unnerved as possible. A wicked scream will make him more likely to goof up as he hurriedly tries to chamber a fresh round. A sound something like a cat caught in a blender is best . . .

Tip #2: Hold your fire and make your first shot count. If the end of your gun barrel is more than three or four feet away from your opponent's body when you pull the trigger, you're too far away. After all, if you charge in, fire, and miss, it will be **you** who will be vulnerable to the screams and the intimidation!

Of course, the type of terrain between you and your opponent will dictate how long it will take you to close the gap on him. If you figure it will take you more than two or three seconds, then I would advise against a banzai charge. Unless your opponent has placed himself in a physically limiting position that will make it hard for him to reload or turn in your direction (such as when he's lying prone or has dug into a bush, in which case he's vulnerable to attack from behind), then three seconds is too long.

Further, if you see that his weapon is lacking a pump, you can figure you'll have a little more time—unless he's got a revolver or a semi-auto type gun, in which case just forget the whole idea!

Making Two Charges

One modification I learned to make in my old style of attack was to break it into two separate charges. If I was close to an opponent but still too far away to cover the ground in the time allowed by the pump guns, I would often wait for him to fire a round, charge in screaming, then pull up a few feet short of him—directly opposite whatever cover he was using. Having me so close to his position would often freak him out, and he would fire his weapon again. If he missed—and he usually did—then he was mine! This technique is diagrammed in the illustrations on the next pages.

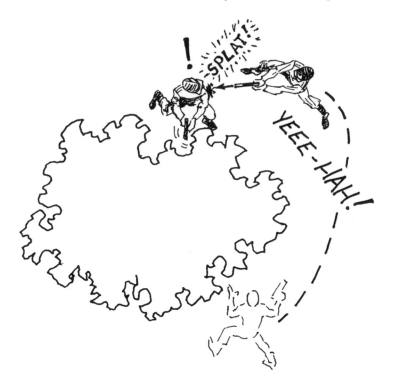

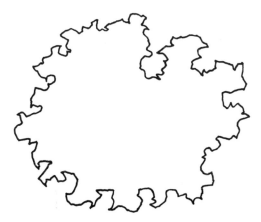

Another perfect time to attempt a banzai charge is when your opponent is changing CO_2 cartridges in his weapon. During this time, if he has no teammates close by to cover him, he will be completely vulnerable, since his weapon is totally useless from the time he removes his old CO_2 cartridge until he inserts and punctures a fresh one.

You can tell when an opponent is changing his CO_2 cartridge by the distinctive hissing sound made by the escaping gas from an old cartridge being removed. If you hear this sound coming from the gun of a solitary player, it's your green light to charge him immediately. If he doesn't run, he'll be such easy pickings that there ought to be a law against it—but there isn't!

Conversely, you've got to watch out for this yourself and make sure you've got protection when you change your own CO_2.

Dealing with Arguments

Be forewarned: the banzai charge causes a lot of arguments. It seems about 80% of the time, your victim, although he knows he's been hit, will immediately start swearing that he has marked *you*. It's a very common misconception. As mentioned earlier, in his panic he probably failed to chamber a round and just shot air, or maybe he simply missed. Often, your opponent will find it incomprehensible that he failed to mark you after firing at such close range, and he will start yelling, "You're hit! You're hit! I *know* I hit you!" I've seen it happen a hundred times.

Of course, as I warned earlier, **never** acquiesce and take yourself out on the basis of your foe's accusations. The proper thing to do is immediately call "Paint check!"

Your opponent will often be a little upset at this point, and you will frequently encounter a degree of hostility in his accusations. The best thing for you to do after you call the paint check is to calmly say, "O. K., if you think you hit me, fine—just show me the paint." If you haven't been hit, he will just inspect you with growing bewilderment and then quietly leave the field, totally intent on nailing your butt in the next game!

I don't know exactly what causes this anger. I guess it's a feeling that the way you screamed at them and shot them at such close range is somehow unfair. But don't let it bother you. Banzai charges are totally fair and completely within the rules of the game. There's nothing "unfair" about playing aggressively! And if you want to win—and have the maximum amount of fun—playing aggressively is the way to go. The rules specifically disallow any type of physical contact between opponents, but anything else goes!

Happy banzaiing!

TACTICAL TIP #8

This one belongs in the Useful-If-You-Can-Get-Them-To-Agree-To-It category: Before their first game, shoot rookies in the back of the leg from a little distance, just to get them used to it. Once they understand that getting shot doesn't really hurt, they can concentrate on playing the game.

Sportsmanship

GOOD SPORTSMANSHIP IS the key to an enjoyable day playing paintball. While you can't control the behavior of your opponents, you can strive to set a shining example for them, and your teammates, to follow.

The most important thing to remember in maintaining exemplary sportsmanship is the same point that has been stressed throughout this book: *it's just a game!* Keeping this very simple fact in mind will do more than anything to help you become the kind of player who is fun to play with and against.

In this book, I've discussed ideas that will help you become a skilled paintball player, and I've cautioned you against such things as blurting out, "I'm hit!" prematurely and thereby unnecessarily removing yourself from a game. And I've encouraged you to do whatever you can to keep your opponents a little intimidated—within the rules, of course.

But rest assured, *nothing* I've said is intended to encourage

you to break or stretch any of the rules, or in any way violate the spirit of the game, just to win. In fact, a "win" gained through dubious methods doesn't fit my—or any other good player's—definition of the word. The old adage is certainly true: if you cheat, you cheat only yourself.

Every truly skilled played I've met has also been, without exception, an exceedingly good sport. It's part of a person's desire to become a superior player in the first place. Anyone who cares about paintball enough, and anyone who enjoys playing so much that he would play enough games to become really skilled, will also care enough about the sport to thoroughly respect its rules.

Of course, just maintaining respect for the rules is certainly not all that good sportsmanship entails. Rather, it encompasses your whole attitude toward the game. The sport involves fun, exercise, the outdoors, camaraderie, and so on, and your attitude should reflect these positive things.

A light-hearted approach in paintball is probably more critical to good play than in most other sports because of the pseudo-aggressive nature of the game. After all, no other sport that I know of is based on the elimination of your opponents! The harshness that such a sport might create needs to be offset by an exaggerated sense of good will and courtesy among the players, as well as constant reminders that it's all just for fun. Like I said earlier, this game will get a little weird if taken too seriously.

Let's consider a few specific examples of good paintball etiquette:

First, obnoxiousness and serious profanity are both definitely taboo. Mild swearing, such as "Dammit, he got me!" is no big sin and won't elicit hard feelings. On the other hand, graphic descriptions of the sexual perversions of your opponent's mother most certainly will! That kind of stuff can lead to big problems and should be strictly out.

On any well-run field, such behavior is grounds for immediate ejection from the game and/or premises. Such conduct is entirely contrary to the spirit of paintball and should not be tolerated.

Another problem: How do you best deal with situations where someone believes they hit you or when you believe you hit someone else? First, consider how often a player is convinced that he marked an opponent when, in fact, he missed him completely. (Remember how I said that 80% of the time after I've eliminated an adversary in a banzai charge, he will *swear* that his dying shot marked me also—when he either missed cleanly or else just shot air?) Keep in mind this tendency for misjudgment as we discuss the proper way to deal with these accusations:

When you think you've hit someone: The proper way to deal with this situation is not to start jumping up and down screaming, "I got you! I got you! I *know* I got you!" You'll look like an idiot, and you might be wrong.

The best way to deal with it is to say, in a non-accusatory tone, "Hey, you behind the bush! Check yourself, please!" If he hollers back, "Sorry, not even close," or maybe, "Naw, just a little spray," simply take his word for it and continue playing. If he answers with something like, "I think you just got a lot of splatter on me. Want to check it?" or if he doesn't respond and you genuinely believe that you've marked him, consider calling a paint check.

The thing you want to avoid is getting into an ever-escalating chain of accusations such as:

"You're hit!"

"Like hell I am!"

"I know damn well you are!"

"Oh yeah, tough guy? Your mother . . ." etc., etc.

Avoid these sophomoric cycles of name-calling either by taking your opponent's word for it, or, if you have genuine doubts, by calling "Paint check!" After all, paint checks were designed to avoid disputes, and they should be used to do so.

When someone thinks he has hit you: The best thing to do is to give a prompt, courteous, honest answer.

If they were way off the mark you can say, "Sorry, missed by a mile!" If they came close, you can say, "Not quite, but a damn good shot!" If you felt a pellet hit you but can't tell whether it broke, get a teammate to check it out or call a paint check and allow your opponent to inspect you. The same applies if you've been hit by heavy splatter.

If you have indeed been shot, promptly announce the fact, put on your elimination vest, and start walking off the field.

If your opponent makes a good shot, then by all means congratulate him on it! A simple, "Nice shot, buddy!" displays good sportsmanship. Usually, other players will follow your good example and respond in kind, thereby making the day more pleasant for all.

When your adversary starts acting like the idiot previously described—being very accusatory and screaming, "I got you! I *know* I got you!" etc.—don't allow yourself to sink to his level. When someone starts a tirade, just calmly respond, "Hey, I didn't feel anything, and I don't think you hit me, but you're welcome to call a paint check and come see for yourself."

This is a very disarming comeback, and you really couldn't offer anything more fair and reasonable. All he can do after such a response is either accept your offer and call a paint check, or take your word for it and get on with the game.

In general, players should try to settle disputes themselves when a judge isn't nearby. However, sometimes this isn't possible, and then it's best for you and the other party to put on your elimination vests and walk together to the nearest judge, rather than allowing yourselves to become embroiled in a heated argument.

The Improving Technology

Another subject I would like to address in this chapter is the ever-"improving" technology of paintball weapons, and the way it has, in my opinion, adversely affected the quality of play.

Back when the sport was first getting started, we were all using Nel-Spots with the awkward left-hand bolt mechanisms. The reloading time was two or three seconds. The CO_2 cartridges had to be replaced every 15 to 20 shots, and it took at least 30 seconds to replace a CO_2. The 10-round paint tubes had to be replaced by pulling out and discarding the old one and then inserting a fresh one.

Though this might seem like a primitive system, it had a definite plus: in those days, arguments were very rare. On the average, one mild disagreement would arise in an entire day of play.

The long period between shots tended to keep the game neat and orderly. You couldn't just "pump away" wildly without running out of pellets and/or CO_2, thus making yourself very vulnerable. In those days, there was much more finesse in the game. You had to pick your shots carefully, and maneuvering on opponents was facilitated by the two to three second "safe time" between shots (which you could count on while scurrying from cover to cover).

Many experienced players, myself included, look back wistfully on the "good old days" of the sport, not because we enjoyed the cumbersome weapons, but because mood-spoiling arguments were so rare. These days, the number of arguments that occur seem to increase in direct proportion to the firepower "improvements" in paintball weapons.

First came the addition of pumps, which greatly reduced the awkwardness of reloading. Then came speed-loaders, which eliminated the need to change paint tubes. Next, someone gave speed-loaders an upward tilt, creating a constant "gravity feed" of the pellets and eliminating the need to tilt the gun barrel down each time you chambered a fresh round. This made the process a bit more sure and perhaps a hair quicker, but still you could fire only so fast because the CO_2 cartridges would "freeze up" and lose their charge if you tried to fire pellets rapidly. Plus, you could fire only so many rounds before your CO_2 ran out.

But then came the next big innovation, "constant air." Somebody, no doubt caught in the throes of paintball mania, developed the idea of carrying a small tank of CO_2 attached to his weapon. Combined with a pump and a large capacity, gravity-fed speed-loader, constant air guns have allowed individuals to achieve and *maintain* fire rates approaching two pellets per second. Compare that to one pellet every three seconds, which we used to be able to get off!

Unfortunately, such rapid fire capabilities have made paintball matches much more chaotic and, inevitably, more argumentative.

Firefights between large groups of players could be confusing even in the old days. Today, if you put two large groups wildly blasting away at one another at two pellets per second, it can be impossible for anyone, including the judges, to figure out what the hell's going on at any given moment.

So you tend to have multiple, vicious, ten-second firefights ending in numerous cries of "Paint check!" Whereupon all sorts of arguments develop along the lines of:

"Terry shot Gary after Harry shot Terry."

"But Jerry shot Harry *before* Harry shot Terry."

"But that's not fair, because Larry and his girlfriend Kari *both* shot Jerry before he shot Harry, who *later* shot Terry before he shot Gary!"

With so many paint pellets whizzing through the air at one time, it can get just about that crazy, believe me. And the problem can be especially acute with large teams playing on fairly open fields, which encourages a lot of firing anyway.

★★★★★★★★★

It's simple and sad: the heated arguments and name-calling make a travesty of the good-natured spirit in which paintball was intended to be played.

I've written this section especially for newer players who probably never experienced the old days when skill, timing, and finesse were much more important for victory. Often these days, whatever team has the latest, most souped-up guns will win. Too bad. Remember, less is often more. Don't allow a mindless quest for greater and greater firepower to corrupt the true spirit of the game.

Some fields, at least on certain days, are not allowing the use of constant air. I believe this is a step in the right direction.

I'm not bemoaning all the new technology. I certainly would hate to give up my pump and my speed-loader, as both solved some very real problems that often detracted from the game. However, I would like to see some sort of ceiling placed on the trend toward more and more "awesome technology," and a greater reliance again placed on the skill factors involved in the sport.

Of course, I don't want this little essay to discourage you from having a wonderful, fun-filled adventure while playing paintball. The good times are still there, believe me.

But advances in weaponry make it more important than ever for all players to exhibit first-rate sportsmanship and fairness at all times. Strive to conduct yourself in way that sets a good example for everyone. And, remember, don't take the damn thing too seriously!

After all, the whole point in playing paintball is to have **fun**. Whatever skills, knowledge, or mental release you might gain from the sport, the primary goal should always be the same—to have a blast and enjoy yourself! You'll achieve this goal easily—and encourage good cheer and camaraderie among all players—if you remember to enjoy paintball for what it is: the best time adults can have this side of the bedroom!

Beyond Capture the Flag:
Scenarios for Paintball Games

by Don Hawthorne

IFIRST BEGAN playing paintball in 1985, and today I try to play at least once a month. After several outings, though, I began to get a little tired of the basic "Capture the Flag" format. I have a great interest in military history and war games, and I thought paintball could provide an enjoyable and safe way to model small unit operations.

After reviewing some books on tactical operations and various small unit missions, I realized that a lot of them could be presented as "missions" for games, either as substitutes for "Capture the Flag" or as modifications to it. These variations lend variety to, and thus greater interest in, paintball. But more importantly, they provide a balance for those times when two teams of very different quality or size oppose one another.

The purpose of this chapter is not to train paramilitary

or terrorist groups, but to give clever, intelligent paintball players more subtle problems and tougher situations than just capturing the enemy's flag. So, whether you're part of an experienced team ready to test your mettle with new challenges, or just a band of eager rookies looking for a little variety, I hope you'll find these suggestions useful. Most important, I hope you have fun with them.

The field I most often play in California has a river deep enough for small rubber rafts, so I have included scenarios that make use of a river. Please note that this river is, at most, waist-deep; I don't advocate playing paintball in water over anybody's head. Not every team or field will have access to the equipment these scenarios present, so feel free to improvise.

I would like to thank Peter Wrenn for introducing me to the sport and always proving to be a dependable partner in a firefight. And my thanks to Bill Barnes, for inviting me to include these notes in his book, for teaching me how to "Banzai!" and for being the "deadliest" player it's ever been my pleasure to hold a hill or wipe-out an enemy strongpoint with. A Rebel Yell to both, and many thanks.

Introduction

I DON'T GET tired of paintball, exactly. Whenever I thought the game was getting a little stale, I modified my style of play. I learned infiltration tactics, how to defend while falling back, and even the dreaded (and fun!) Banzai Charge. To make the game better, I had to get better at it, and, in all modesty, I got pretty good. Not terrific—not even what you would call a "pro"—but pretty good.

Despite my increasing skill, I often felt there was something missing. Eventually, I figured out what it was. On all the fields I played on, the day went something like this:

Side A goes to one end of the field. Side B goes to the other end. They play Capture the Flag. Switch fields, play Capture the Flag. Switch sides on the new field, play Capture the Flag. Single Flag, Double Flag, Free for All Capture the Flag, Total Elimination Capture the Flag.

I think you get the picture.

Don't get me wrong—Capture the Flag has a lot going for it. For one thing, it's almost universally played, so everybody knows the rules. It's perfect for familiarizing rookies with paintball in general and for tuning-up old hands who may need to get back to basics when rusty or overconfident. As far as I know, it (or something like it) is the only game played at national tournaments. And to be fair, Capture the Flag is, in my opinion, far superior to gun-slinging matches whose only purpose is to rack-up as high a body count as possible. Still . . .

Haven't you, from time to time, gotten a little bored with always knowing basically what the enemy team was going to do? You may not be sure how they're going to come after your flag or try to eliminate you and your comrades, but you know that they will try. In short, the enemy's objective is always known, as is the enemy's force strength and general starting area. You also know that the team with the bigger budget is going to have more ammo and maybe better weapons, but that's the sort of thing you just have to live with if you want to play.

The purpose of this chapter is to let players and field proprietors know that paintball is open to innovations that are easy and inexpensive to implement, safe, and best of all, fun. Many fields already have villages, bunkers, and emplacements. Some even have mock-up tanks, but not all field proprietors can afford such extras. (Indeed, some fields are not suited to them. A field that was mostly "jungle" certainly would have no use for "tanks," and a field out in the desert probably doesn't need rubber rafts.)

The Problems with Capture the Flag

Problems with paintball are not with the field but with the game played on it: Capture the Flag.

The first problem with Capture the Flag is obvious: its name. There's really only one objective—the flag. Both teams know what the other wants, and worst of all, they usually know right where it is. The only uncertainty lies in the route of enemy approach.

A second problem is that teams are usually of equal size. Though walk-on players are often used to fill-out the ranks of the smaller group, they can cause a total lack of coordination and unit cohesion. And since the opponents know how big the force opposing them is, certain inevitable techniques arise:

The smaller team might dig-in against a larger team or a team believed to be more talented (a potentially fatal error). Or the smaller team may decide to try to "kamikaze" the larger one (a definitely fatal error). Perhaps the bigger team will decide to attack in a "human wave" assault. This can be fun once, but it gets dull by the third or fourth game of the day. And there isn't much reason to brag about it at work the rest of the week, since it's neither brave nor clever.

The final, worst problem is that paintball could be in danger of stagnation. New players discover it every day, of course, and old hands learn new tricks, so it's doubtful that the sport will wither any time soon. But all teams play according to the same basic formula: a base group is left to guard the flag station, and an assault group goes out to attack and capture the enemy flag. While this is tactically sound, it can become exceedingly dull. It's the same thing over and over again, and every team I've played with or against is guilty of it.

The problem is not that teams lack imagination, but that they lack incentive to change or develop new tactics. Capture the Flag is basically the same game cavemen played when stealing meat or women from neighboring tribes.

Understand, if the day's efforts were going to guarantee me a date (or even a steak), I'd say fine, no problem—stick with what works (light-eyed brunettes and medium rare, if anybody's listening). But the object is always to Capture the Damned Flag, and that is precisely the problem. Most teams out there have been playing so long that they are expert in doing just that.

So, if you and your team are so almighty awesome, let's see what *else* you can do. Consistency is nice—if you can capture a flag 100 times a day, great. But *versatility*, in my opinion, is far superior. And that's what the following scenarios are about.

Scenario One:
Supply Train

Extra Materials Required: Three large ice chests (or similar burden).

Victory Conditions: The larger team must transport three "Supply Bins" from Point A to Point B within the time limit of the game, while suffering fewer than three times as many casualties as its opponent.

Comments: The important part of this scenario isn't the ice chests; it's the casualty rate. To keep casualties low, the larger team will have to use effective reconnaissance and screening techniques while transporting the chests. Since a good-sized ice chest requires two hands to carry, and since most paintguns also require two hands to operate, the transporting team usually must use two men per chest. If the players are in good shape, add more difficulty: pack the chests with sand, bricks, or whatever. If it's the last game of the day and the field proprietor agrees, you could even weigh them down with beer—to be consumed *off* the field, of course.)

This scenario is good for pitting a larger team against a smaller, perhaps more experienced, force.

Another variant would be to allow for the capture of the ice chests (treat them as mobile Flag Stations, but capturing one or all does not end the game). A captured ice chest could count as three eliminated enemy team members, for instance. These points should be awarded only to the team that has the chests at game's end, and should not be awarded to the team that started the game with them if it is the larger team.

Scenario Two:
Relief Force

Extra Materials Required: None.

Game Set-Up: One third of a team is allowed extended time (perhaps 10 to 20 minutes) to place themselves in defensible positions within a small area chosen by the referee. The players in this force are issued ten rounds of ammunition and one CO_2 cartridge per person.

Once in place, this unit is then surrounded by the entire opposing team, at a range chosen by the referee. Eliminated players of this surrounded force (only) may give their remaining ammo to their surviving teammates before leaving the field. The remaining two-thirds of this team starts at the far end of the field from their encircled teammates.

Victory Conditions: The teammates of the surrounded unit must break through the enemy and evacuate as many of their trapped buddies back to their side of the field as possible. They may bring extra ammo and CO_2 to re-supply the trapped unit should they reach it in time. Surrounded players fight normally at all times until eliminated. If the relief force brakes through with supplies, eliminated players may no longer give their ammo to teammates.

A variation of this scenario assumes the encircled troops have captured some item such as Secret Plans, represented by a briefcase or a notebook. To win, the relief force must keep this item from falling into the hands of the surrounding team. If the surrounding team captures the item and returns it to its flag station, they win. Also, surrounded players alive at the end of the game can be assigned a point value to make their rescue even more important.

Comments: This scenario is basically a large-scale version of something that happens a lot in regular paintball: players get ahead of the main force or lag behind, enemy teams pin them down, and they have to be rescued. On this scale, however, the surrounded players feel like the Germans at Stalingrad, the Americans at Bastogne, or the French at Dien Bien Phu. The difference is, paintball players *know* help is on the way.

Scenario Three:
Delaying Action

Extra materials required: None.

Game Set-Up: This is a scenario for two teams of very different size. The larger team begins at one end of the field, with the smaller team immediately adjacent. The smaller team must make a fighting withdrawal back to its flag station at the opposite end of the field.

Victory Conditions: The smaller team must reach its own flag station while keeping its casualties to fewer than half the number suffered by the larger team.

Comments: This can be a deceptively tough assignment, considering the sizes of the teams and relative experience of their members. Generally, the smaller team should be more experienced. Another factor to consider is the casualty ratio. Some players must stay behind and sacrifice themselves to aid their team's retreat. Think of it as evolution in action.

Some Variants: The larger team may deploy in a screen or in "pockets." The retreating team must pass through the screen or between the pockets. In this case, the larger team should be allowed a few minutes set-up time prior to game start.

Or: The retreating team must inflict twice as many casualties on their pursuers as they themselves suffer, and they must do it before they reach their flag station. In this case, there is no time limit to the game. It ends the moment any member of the retreating team reaches his flag station.

Scenario Four:
Prisoners

Extra Materials Required: None.

Victory Conditions: The attacking team must "capture" at least four member of the defending team. "Prisoners" are enemies who have been hit only in the arms or the legs. Hits to the body or head eliminate the player from the game. Note that only members of the *defending* team can be "wounded" and thus become "prisoners." Any hit on a member of the attacking team eliminates that player from the game.

Once hit, "prisoners" must also be tagged by an attacker to be captured. Simply marking them with paint does not make them prisoners.

Special rules apply to such "wounded" men. Once hit in the arms or legs, they may not fire, nor may they move unless their teammates carry them. They must stay in place, calling out: "Prisoner!" Once enemy players reach their position, the wounded are considered "captured" and may move normally, but they may not run away. They may only move with their captors, and they must have a guard with them at all times. If his captors are eliminated, the prisoner may return to play as if he had never been marked.

After prisoners have been captured, they must be brought to the enemy flag station and are worth five "kills" apiece to the capturing team. Then, prisoners must leave the game for good. The flag station is treated as a neutral area in this scenario; no combat is allowed in or around it.

The game ends when four prisoners have been turned in, or when the time limit is reached.

Scenario Five:
Paratroop Drop

Extra Material Required: Blindfolds or large-billed caps. (No, you do not need a plane. Of course, if you want to jump out of one to play this game, go right ahead.)

Game Set-Up: Before the game, the "Para" team should form three or four squads of equal number. Split these squads into groups of two or three players. These groups are then dispersed over a wide area by the judges. The players in each group stay together, but the groups are spread out, with at least 50 feet between groups. The groups should not know the locations of their comrades. They should be blindfolded while being escorted to their starting position (or use large-billed caps and keep their heads down). The important thing is to make each group feel isolated when the game begins.

The area over which the judges deploy the "Paras" represents the "Drop Zone," and since paratroopers tend to land in dispersed straight lines, the "Para" team should be deployed accordingly. Cover density between the groups shouldn't be too thick, since paratroops usually jump into fairly open areas, and the groups will need to have some idea of the whereabouts of their fellow players to have any chance of surviving the first five minutes of this scenario. Because . . .

The defending team is allowed to deploy first, and they should be allowed to see as much as they can without actually running around. They must pick defensive spots before the "Paras" are deployed, and they must stay there until the game begins.

Victory Conditions: The "Paratrooper" team must consolidate its groups back into the squads established before the start of the game, and then capture the enemy flag position. It need not return the flag to a particular place; just capture the defender's flag station.

Prepare a distinctive arm band or tag for each squad to identify survivors when the game ends. The "Paras" must have at least one surviving member *from each squad* at game's end, or they lose—whether they capture the enemy flag station or not.

A particularly nasty variant for this scenario is to allow eliminated "Paras" to re-join the game after they have spent a certain amount of time off the field. (They represent stragglers who reach the battlefield late.)

To aid the defense, allow them to pick the placement of their flag station without informing the judges of its whereabouts. Or, allow the defending team to move its flag station around the field in this scenario. Remember: judges may deploy the "Paras" anywhere they choose, including right in the middle of the defender's flag station! These sacrificial lambs aren't likely to win the game, since the "Para" players must re-form their squad to win and capture the enemy flag station, but they will make the first few minutes of the battle very interesting.

This scenario gets pretty ugly in terms of casualties suffered by the "Paras," but some good things happen, too. The most bumbling team will develop a swagger and *esprit de corps* when they're told they are a group of "paratroopers." Believe it or not, their performance even improves commensurately. Go figure.

Comments: Judges should be aware that dispersing the "Paras" too widely, or deliberately deploying them in poor positions, will have the same result as such actions would in reality. The "Paras" will be wiped out.

If the field proprietors have maps avilable of the playing area, let the "Para" players use them. They'll probably need all the help they can get . . .

Scenario Six:
Assaulting a Fortification

Extra Materials Required: A pillbox, maybe two. Don't be discouraged—they aren't that tough to make or find. The best kind, because it's easily moved, is made from a 4' x 8' sheet of ¾" plywood. Cut three firing slits about 3" high by 18" wide length-wise along the plywood and about a foot in from one side. This side now becomes the "top." Prop the plywood between a couple of trees or make braces for it, and you have a pillbox.

Game Set-Up: The playing field should have very little cover and, if possible, a dominating terrain feature such as a hill or ridge. Place the "pillbox" at the top of this terrain feature. (For purposes of this scenario, the pillbox must have an open back.) Some fields already have pillboxes or other strong points: cement culverts, old automobiles, even grounded water towers. But most of the places I've played have made these structures to reduce their fields of fire in the interest of play balance. Sometimes their firing ports are even facing away from the main route of approach. This doesn't exactly make for a fair game, since the assaulting players never have to learn how to overcome what should be a fearsome defensive emplacement. Guarding the main (or even the only) routes of approach is, after all, what pillboxes are for.

The pillbox shouldn't hold more than four people. Anybody inside who is eliminated may be replaced by a teammate from outside the pillbox as the game progresses. The open back of the pillbox may be guarded as securely as the defending players wish. The remaining defenders should be given a short time to dig-in around the pillbox's perimeter.

Field boundaries should be established to allow only one route of approach for assaulting the pillbox, with very little room to manuever to the sides or rear. Natural boundaries for such consideration are best but not always available, so feel free to make the best use of what you've got.

Victory Conditions: The attacking team must carry out its assault on the fortification from the front only, preferably uphill. They must clear and occupy the enemy pillbox (or pillboxes) to win. Any other result is a win for the defending team.

Some Variants: In one variation, the attackers don't have to attack the pillbox. Instead, they only have to get past it, bypassing the enemy strongpoint on their way to another objective. They should have a very limited time in which to do this, and should be under constraints to keep their casualties low—say, no more than ⅓ of the men they start with.

Another variation: Create two pillboxes, with or without complimentary fields of fire—very bad for the attackers!

If the defending team has any rapid-fire or auto-fire weapons, put them in the pillbox. The attackers should heavily outnumber them—or be very, very good.

Comments: You can play this scenario with a few guys in a high rock formation. (Running into such a situation is what gave me the idea.) In fact, on fields with such terrain, this situation usually arises. But most fields also have cover. In reality, pillboxes are often made at bleak, defoliated areas that swiftly turn into killing fields during enemy advance attempts. As a result, attackers without artillery or air support will bypass such positions whenever possible.

In game terms, the best part about having the fortification on a hill is its psychological effect. People simply hate to march uphill against a wall that shoots. But the team that can bring itself to do so, and do it sucessfully, can be justly proud of itself.

Scenario Seven:
Raid

Extra Materials Required: None, unless a village area is available or can be simulated without much trouble.

Game Set-Up: At least half of the defending team must deploy in the village or in a bivouac area at one end of the playing field. This half of the defense may not leave the area until they are attacked by the raiding force.

The raiding force starts at the opposite end of the field. They must choose some area in the middle of the field as an "evacuation" area. Upon reaching this area, they may leave as many men as they wish, but must leave at least four. The remainder of their force may then proceed to the village to carry out the raid.

Victory Conditions: The raiding force must make its way through the outer perimeter of defense troops, attack the village, and inflict a certain number of casualties (established by the judges prior to the game). The raiders must then fall back to their "evacuation" area, re-form their team, and return to their starting point at their end of the field. If the "evacuation" area has been overrun by the defense, the raiders must re-take it before they can re-form their team.

Variants: This scenario was designed originally for a field with a small river. The evacuation point was the riverbank, where the attacking team was to leave small rubber rafts to carry out the evacuation. With only a few rafts, the raiding force had to escape in shifts, and this alone made the

scenario very exciting indeed. (Scenario Nine is an expanded version of this situation.)

To make this scenario more challenging for the offense, do not allow the raiding force to suffer more than a certain level of casualties, or no more than one raider for every three or four defenders. Or, stipulate that after reaching the evacuation area, the attackers cannot suffer any further casualties before reaching their flag station, or they lose.

Or, put a specific item or target in the village which must be captured or eliminated in order for the attackers to win.

Comments: In this scenario, effective reconnaissance techniques become critical both for attacker and defender. The attacker needs to find the enemy camp and hit it before its guards find him. He must then fall back to his evacuation point before it is overrun and make his escape. Players will have to perform effective screening manuevers in attempts to hit the enemy hard where he is weak, and avoid having the same thing done to them. The defenders, with players concentrated in the village until attacked, seem like cattle in a pen at first, but this force amounts to a "strategic reserve," which can prove to be a hornet's nest of trouble for the raiders unless they carry out their end of the operation effectively.

Scenario Eight:
River Rats

Extra Materials Required: Inflatable rubber rafts, two- to four-man size, no more than one for every ten members of the River Rat team. And, of course, a river.

Game Set-Up: The River Rats team must escort the rafts from one end of a stream or river to the other. They may take them either up- or downstream as they wish (or as the judges deem best for purposes of play balance or safety). At least two of their teammates must be in each raft at all times. If both occupants of a raft are eliminated, the raft must be re-crewed. Other team members may accompany the rafts in the stream, or they may need to pull them against the current. It goes without saying that the rafts may not, under any conditions, be powered. The rest of the River Rats may "escort" the rafts by traveling along the riverbank with the rafts. Or, they may be deployed in any other way the River Rats team desires.

Victory Conditions: The River Rats must get the rafts up- or downstream without losing more men than the enemy team. The enemy team will comprise a "harassing force," moving along the river bank ahead of the River Rats, sniping at them as they go.

Comments: This scenario will teach the River Rats how to guard their flanks. Using the river as an uncompromising route of travel forces the two teams into limited routes of attack and defense. While the River Rats are learning how to guard their flanks (established by the riverbank), the

Harassing Force will be learning ambush and infiltration techniques. The longer the river, the tougher this gets for both sides. It's also a great scenario for really hot days.

TACTICAL TIP #9

Store your unused paint pellets in a cool, dry place. Keeping them in a sealed baggie is a good idea. Pellets have a shelf life of only a few months, so try not to get overstocked. If you notice that the paint in the pellets has settled, shake them a little or roll them around in a bowl to solve the problem.

Scenario Nine:
Evacuation

Extra Materials Required: Rafts and a river, if you've got them. Otherwise, any area where a large amount of people can entrench with their backs to a wall, with only one route of escape.

Game Set-Up: The defending team holds an exposed beach-head/staging area on a riverbank, or perhaps at the base of a hillside or ravine. The enemy team is assaulting this position.

Victory Conditions: The defending team must evacuate as many of its people as possible via raft (or other means as decided by the judges) to its own Base Camp at another end of the field. Players who are marked with body- or head-shots leave the field as they would normally. Players marked by arm- or leg-shots are "wounded" and must be evacuated by raft (or other means). If they walk back to the Judge's Area or Base Camp, they are counted as "kills" for the attacking team. Such "wounded" players may not use their weapons, but otherwise they're still in the game.

The attacking team must attempt to overrun the evacuation zone, cut-off the defending team's escape route, and then eliminate the defenders—while suffering under 50% casualties.

Variants: The attacking team must completely wipe-out the defending team to win. Any non-evacuated players still at the evacuation point at game's end result in a win for the evacuating team. Evacuated players count as three kills for the evacuating team.

Or try this: Escaping units on the river (or in the evacuation "pipeline") cannot be attacked. Treat the river or escape route as a "free zone" for the evacuating player only.

Comments: This scenario demonstrates the vulnerability of massed troops, particularly on beachheads. The attacker can afford to give no quarter, and the defender must decide which troops to leave to cover escapes and how many to evacuate while doing so.

Other Innovations

In addition to these ten scenarios, field proprietors all over the country have created countless paintball innovations. For example, Bruce Winship of Firepower in Moorpark, CA, was the first field proprietor in my experience to use the following variants:

MEDICS: One or more players on a team are given white t-shirts to wear over their camouflage gear. Each t-shirt has a large red cross on the front and back, identifying the wearers as "medics" for their teammates only. Medics function in the following manner:

Marked players do not leave the field. Instead, they lie where they are hit and do nothing but shout "Medic!" as often as necessary. If one of their Medics can get to them and tag any part of their body, they immediately return to the game. Medics hit by paint are eliminated, unless there is another Medic still in the game. If a Medic who has been hit is tagged by another Medic, the painted Medic removes his red cross t-shirt and returns to the game as a regular player.

PARATROOPS: Bruce Winship also put paratroops into a game by letting our team know that our opponents had a "special edge" to balance the play. Their edge: they could bring their "dead" men back into the game in our rear area, forward of our flag station but behind our main assault force. And each returnee shouted "Paratrooper!" at the top of his lungs. Very unnerving!

Bruce Winship also uses several of his own game scenarios at Firepower, and he and his wife April run one of the most enjoyable fields I've ever played on.

Players in New England should try Survival South in West Greenwich, RI—one of the largest fields with some of the toughest terrain I've ever seen.

Cover on the Survival South field is dense and plentiful. The terrain is varied, and surprises can be very nasty, making the excitement level consistently high. Survival South is run in an extremely courteous, professional manner by Mitch Ribak and Mike Shein.

Both of these fields lend themselves to fascinating variations, and they provide a consistently challenging environment for good old Capture the Flag.

I hope you will try these scenarios and suggestions at least a few times. If one side seems too powerful in a scenario, switch sides and see how the other team does. Mix and match scenarios and victory conditions, and don't hesitate to include capturing the flag as a condition of victory.

I believe that the best way to increase enjoyment of paintball is to increase its variety. The more varied the tasks presented to the players, the more varied the tactics they will develop to accomplish them. And the more you learn about the game, the more fun it is.

Approach these scenarios with an open mind, and try to understand the tactical concepts they teach. The skills they can impart in reconnaissance, infiltration, screening, and all the other little tricks of the trade will assist in playing the standard Capture the Flag version. I believe that playing one or two of these scenarios per day will reward innovative, skillful teams and will create a higher level of excitement and variety for all players. You might even reach such a level of professionalism in your play that you don't mind losing your flag to an enemy.

Or even such a level that you never lose it again.

Battle Plans of the Allied Special Forces

NOT LONG AGO, I had the opportunity to organize a new paintball team in Greensboro, NC. I chose 14 players from the area, and we called ourselves the Allied Special Forces. For our first tournament, I created an informal (but effective) set of "battle plans" for the team. Since they distill the key points I've tried to express in this book, I decided to present them below, with the hope that you can apply them to your team's situation:

Partial Roster

Mike Ahauna	Eugene Brown
Ed Pearson	Butch Warren
Randall Atkins	Jim Gwynn
Steve Raeford	Vann Warren
Bill Barnes	Sam King
Andy Reed	Gee Whiz
Ron Betts	Guy Miller
Doug Tate	

Attackers:

1. You must maintain momentum! Remember the words of Andrew Reed, great American paintballer: "If you want to remain in one spot, bring your tombstone with you!"

2. We have one goal, and one goal only: to **capture** and **return** the enemy flag. We have only 45 minutes to accomplish this. We either succeed or die trying. No one comes off the field alive without a flag capture.

3. We'll be attacking down the wire (the boundary). Reasons: it cuts our worry area from 180° to 90°, and it facilitates *fast* movement.

4. We must be especially alert for side-door bogeys.

5. Point men should engage, shout "Bogey!" and say its location, and lay down a **barrage** of suppressive fire.

6. Flankers immediately push both sides, if possible. If you're unseen by the enemy, you may choose to remain silent briefly. Regardless, at least 75% of the team must make a constant racket (exchanging info, Rebel Yells, "Allies!," etc.).

7. We'll be hitting the enemy hard, fast, and (probably) with numerical superiority. We must take full advantage of this. Once we break their lines and get them on the run, we must **keep** them on the run! We must keep them off-balance and give them no time whatsoever to re-group. Such an attack style will give us a big psychological advantage. Remember, paintball is largely a mind-game.

8. An appropriate analogy for #7 above is that we must play paintball the way Mike Tyson fights—with controlled fury. (Our style will be hard and fast, but not kamikaze.)

9. Upon our arrival at the enemy flag station, we must immediately flank to both sides.

10. We must steal the enemy flag at the first opportunity. (The first flag capture will earn us 10 points.)

11. If surviving manpower permits, we must always ambush a secured enemy flag station with at least two players. (It's strategic ground that we had to fight for, and there's no sense giving it back to the enemy, especially since they might be returning with **our** flag!)

12. We will return with a captured flag using the same route that we advanced on, with the flag carrier closely escorted and at least one point man leading the way.

13. We owe it to the out-gunned defense to **attack fast!**

    P.S. Our code name is *Delta*.

Defenders:

1. We'll have six players on defense, divided into three, two-man squads: *Alpha, Bravo,* and *Charlie.*

2. Mission: To sprint at the beginning of games to a point near mid-field, and then spread out in a picket line across the 75% of the field not covered by *Delta. Charlie* will be the squad closest to *Delta,* and *Alpha* the farthest away. *Bravo* will be the defensive command squad.

3. A large part of your job will be to survey the field and report what you see regarding enemy troop strength and location to *Delta.*

4. For intimidation purposes, fire at the enemy from a distance.

5. If both fire teams are still alive and need to retreat, they should do so in a leapfrog pattern.

6. Retreat quickly, attain solid cover, whirl around, and try to catch the enemy exposed.

7. Don't forget the old "leaky CO_2" trick. It might just work!

8. If you're able to retain your mid-field positions, periodically send a runner or two back to check the flag.

9. Code phrase for falling back to the flag: "We're (I'm) out of ammo!"

10. Around the 35-minute mark, any defenders not engaged in a firefight **must** go after the enemy flag.

11. You will be fighting a delayed action, so try to sell yourselves dear . . .

Charlie Squad's Special Assignment: *Charlie* may be assigned by either *Delta* or *Bravo* to join with *Delta* as part of the flag assault group. If *Charlie* goes with *Delta*, it will probably have the job of protecting *Delta's* inside flank. *Charlie* must announce its arrival to *Delta* loudly!

All Allies:

1. Constant communication between all squads is essential!

2. Your team name is **Allies**. Use it liberally, both for communication purposes and as a battle cry.

3. A team member alive at the end of the game doesn't mean squat! Only total points for the tournament matter. We must capture and return the enemy flag, or die trying . . .

4. Every player should wear a watch. Mark the time at the start of each game and keep track of the time remaining.

5. Paintball is a strenuous sport. Exercise during the week, stretch out before the game, and wear lightweight shoes. Remember, we've got to play all day for two days in a row, and tournaments have been won and lost by a few seconds. Wear knee pads if you have them, and don't be afraid to get down in the dirt!

6. Carry plenty of paint and CO_2. Fire tons of paint! If all you can see is an enemy's shoelace, shoot at it!

7. This is **tournament** play. No surrenders, to offers to surrender, nothing wimpy.

8. Usually, you should abandon any position when you catch a "bouncer." Definitely abandon if you don't know where it came from!

9. We should maintain a sense of camaraderie on our team. Let's huddle-up before the game and give a battle cry! We must fight together and protect one another like we're brothers. We will win or lose **together.** If we lose, there will be no post-game accusations and finger-pointing. We should accept the loss and realize that we did the best we could. Then, we'll have a constructive discussion of what went wrong and enter the next contest in high spirits!

10. Any great paintball team is greater than the sum of its parts, thanks to **teamwork**. Don't forget it!

One final note, Allies: shit happens!

Nothing ever goes exactly (or even close) to plan. Nothing here is written in stone. You can usually get an accurate picture of a game's status by noting the time and the duration and location of firefights, and then figuring in information from teammates. Pay attention, and constantly think about how something might effect the game's outcome—and respond accordingly.

The biggest reason I've written these battle plans is to open your minds and get you thinking. Play loose. Don't be afraid to take advantage of opportunities as they present themselves. Always be aware of the time remaining. Communicate constantly. Adapt and overcome.

Let's be on time. Let's be prepared. Let's be good sports. Let's kick some butt! Let's win this damn tournament!

Team Names

JUST FOR KICKS, and in no particular order, here are some team names that I've heard in my years of playing paintball. By the way, if you'd like your team's name included, write me (c/o Mustang Publishing, P.O. Box 3004, Memphis, TN 38173) and I'll try to list it in future editions.

Allied Special Forces
Fighting 69th
The Bushmen
Bushmasters
Headhunters
Wolverines
Peacekeepers
Ranger Elite
The Untouchables
Varmint Cong
Wolfpack
Zoo Squad
F-Troop
Hogan's Heroes
Sting

Hillbillies
NATO (Northern Alleghany
  Treaty Organization)
Colonial Marines
Birds of Prey
Crow Warriors
Kansas City Wrecking Crew
Reagan Youth
The Swarm
Nuclear Waste
Waffen Elite
Gang Green
Dirty Dozen
Iron Cross
Legion of Doom

WELL, HONEY, WHAT SHOULD WE CALL THEM?

First Strike
Sudden Death
Wasters
The Eliminators
Havok!
Dac Attack
Desert Rats
Vipers
The Good, the Bad, and
  the Uglies
Clete's Eletes
Krash Krew
Combat Crew
Motley Crew
James Gang
Panic
Pillagers
Nightmare
Land Sharks
Buckaroos
Iron Men

Wasteland Mutants
Mercenaries
Guns for Hire
Tippmann Bulldogs
Dream Warriors
Civil Warriors
Cotton Mouths
Paintball Army
NBC Destroyers
Strike Force Rangers
Those Guys Mercenary Service
Border Bandits
Fine Young Cannibals
Birnam Foresters
Florida Gator Men
Fayette'nam
Devil Pups
Wild Geese (*1987 N.S.G.
  Champions*)
Chuck
Rock Creek Commandos

Bladerunners
S.P.L.A.T. (Survival Players Lunatic Attack Team)
Widow Makers
Santa Barbarians
K.M.A. (Kill 'M All)
Long Range Reconnaissance Patrol (LRRPs)
Buck County Warriors
Software Station Survivors
Green Machine
Strike Force
Master Blaster
Mutant Ninja
Iron Turtles
Saratoga Timber Rattlers
Tree Dancers
Nashville Ridgerunners
Timberlords
Grave Diggers
The Yuppie Hunters
Renegades
Urban Gorillas
No Name Team
Navarone Armageddon
Navarone Apocalypse
Unknown Rebels
Over-the-Hill Gang
Rampage
Mothers of Destruction
Terminators
Predators
Tasmanian Devils
Mary's Lambs
Jerry's Kids (*they played like it!*)
T.I.G.E.R.S. (Terrorists who Infiltrate and Garrote Enemy Recruits)
82nd Beerborne
Captain Suds and the Brew Patrol
Hosers
Weekend Warriors
The Wackos
F.A.R.T. (Friends Are Rare Treats)
Passing Wind
Lester's Molesters
MoFo's
Assailants

Highly Irregulars
Purple Haze
Great American Commando Club
The Force
Boonie Rats (*a great bunch of guys from Texas!*)
The Red-Eyed Knights
Black Knights (*West Point cadets*)
Direct Hits
Rough Riders
Black Sheep
Raccoons
Rambozos
The Maniacs
The Earl Scheibs (*motto: "We will paint any team, any color, for $29.95. No extras."*)
Dismanglers
Descending Angels
Wannabees
Face Us Face Death
Take No Prisoners
Merchants of Death
Lawmen
Outlaws
Flying Lizards
Blue Blaze Irregulars
No Mercy
Fuquay-Varina Nightmare
Delta Force
The Little Rascals (*motto: "Check yourself, Spanky!"*)
Devil's Brigade
Satan's Soldiers
The Bastards from Hell
Awesome Splatmasters
Ground Zero
Wild Geese Recon
Grove City Gut-Rippers
Death R Us
Grimm Reapers
Vendetta
The Saigon Psychos
Walking Dead
Bushwackers
Ballbusters

Deadly Force
Diaper Patrol
Vigilantes
War Lords
Team Dorsai (*paintball knights*)
Icemen
Taipans (*Australian team*)
Splat Rats
Death Rangers
Oregon Ballbusters
Lords of Discipline
Mickey's Jihad (*Disneyland's team!*)
Capital Punishment (*from Texas,*
of course)
Kamikaze Shooters (*mostly Asians,*
all with constant air)
Delta Dogs

Mad Dogs
Mad Dog Rangers
Yard Dogs
Junkyard Dogs
Mohican Mag Dogs
Norwegian Slime Dogs
Dirty Dogs from Hell
Hell Hounds
Homely Hounds
Rabid Rabbits
Screamin' Weasels
Weasel Slayers
War Pigs
Hello Kitty
Contra Band
Bodycount
Mau Mau
Splatoon

And at last, but certainly not least, a group of great guys and party animals who call themselves The Taxi Drivers from Hell—soon to be known as The Beavers from Outer Space!